Adventurous

wom

OTHER BOOKS BY DORCAS S. MILLER

Stars of the First People: Native American Star Myths and Constellations

Kayaking the Maine Coast: A Paddler's Guide to Day Trips from Kittery to Cobscook

Rescue: Stories of Survival from Land and Sea

Backcountry Cooking: From Pack to Plate in 10 Minutes

Good Food for Camp and Trail: A Guide to Planning and Preparing Delicious All-Natural Meals Outdoors

Track Finder: A Guide to Mammal Tracks, Eastern North America

Berry Finder: A Guide to Fleshy Fruits, Eastern North America

Winter Weed Finder: A Guide to Pods, Seeds, and Dried Flowers, Eastern North America

Adventurous women

THE INSPIRING LIVES OF NINE EARLY OUTDOORSWOMEN

BY DORCAS S. MILLER

PRUETT PUBLISHING COMPANY
BOULDER, COLORADO

Printed in the United States

09 08 07 06 05 04 03 02 01 00   5 4 3 2 1

The following institutions and photographer have generously granted permission to reproduce these photographs: cover, chapter openers, pp. 134 and 138— from Mary Jobe Akeley Collection and reprinted courtesy of Mystic River Historical Society, Inc., Mystic Connecticut; p. 2—courtesy of Paul Mozell, Wakefield, Massachusetts; p. 16—courtesy of the Vancouver Public Library (E. Pauling Johnson, #9430); p. 152—courtesy of the Bancroft Pictorial Collection, Bancroft Library, University of California, Berkeley, California (Marion Randall Parsons portrait #24).

Library of Congress Cataloging-in-Publication Data

Miller, Dorcas S., 1949–
    Adventurous women : the inspiring lives of nine early
outdoorswomen / Dorcas S. Miller.
        p.   cm.
    Includes bibliographical references (p.) and index.
    ISBN 0-87108-864-9 (alk. paper)
    1. Women adventurers—United States Biography. 2. Women
adventurers—Canada Biography. 3. Women—United States Biography.
4. Women—Canada Biography. 5. United States Biography. 6. Canada
Biography.   I. Title.
CT9970.M55   1999
920.72'0973—dc21   99-35746
                                                          CIP

Cover and book design by Julie N. Long
Book composition by Lyn Chaffee

TO JEAN HOEKWATER,

A FELLOW ADVENTURER AND A WOMAN OF GREAT COURAGE,

AND TO AUNT LOUISE,

WHO HAD ADVENTURES APLENTY IN HER NINETY-SEVEN YEARS

TABLE OF CONTENTS

PREFACE   *ix*

ACKNOWLEDGMENTS   *xvii*

CHAPTER 1: ENCOURAGING LADIES TO CAMP
   MARTHA WHITMAN (1840–1884)   *1*

CHAPTER 2: THE SONG MY PADDLE SINGS
   E. PAULINE JOHNSON, TEKAHIONWAKE (1862–1913)   *17*

CHAPTER 3: CONQUERING MOUNT HUASCARAN
   ANNIE SMITH PECK (1850–1935)   *37*

CHAPTER 4: A THIRST FOR ADVENTURE
   DORA KEEN (1871–1963)   *55*

CHAPTER 5: A TENDERFOOT NO LONGER
   GRACE GALLATIN SETON (1872–1959)   *81*

CHAPTER 6: THE WOMAN HOMESTEADER
   ELINORE PRUITT STEWART (1876–1933)   *99*

CHAPTER 7: ADVENTURES OF AN AUTHOR
   MARY ROBERTS RINEHART (1876–1958)   *119*

CHAPTER 8: MY QUEST IN THE CANADIAN ROCKIES
   MARY JOBE (1878–1966)   *135*

CHAPTER 9: DWELLING CLOSE TO THE HEART OF THINGS
   MARION RANDALL PARSONS (1880–1953)   *153*

APPENDIX: CHRONOLOGY   *169*

NOTES   *181*

BIBLIOGRAPHY   *189*

INDEX   *197*

PREFACE

I had been on the river for a month, paddling, lining, and portaging the Dubawnt with five companions. We had flown into Ivanhoe Lake, north of Alberta, and were headed to Baker Lake, deep in Canada's Northwest Territories. On this day we had carried around a waterfall and reloaded the canoes with the intent of running the shallow water below. We paddled out into the wide river and ran down the center. Suddenly, the world gave way and the rushing green water carried us toward a ledge that stretched right and left to infinity. What looked like a shoal revealed itself to be a precipitous drop.

There was no time to think, no time to panic. Paddling on instinct, I headed toward a sketchy line that might possibly take us through. My partner and I, paddling as one person, slid through the roiling water. Moments later, still charged with adrenalin, I found myself at the bottom of the rapid, canoe upright, with surprisingly little water splashing between my feet.

Slowly the world widened, and I saw that the other boats had made it, too. We were all safe, if shaken and soggy. It would have been a race with hypothermia if anyone had capsized. Although it was early in the day, we paddled to the riverbank and set up camp. I thought about the stunning vastness of the land—from horizon to horizon not even a tree broke the view. The other world was incomparably faraway.

The seven-week Dubawnt River trip in 1975 left an indelible mark. The trip engendered within me a thirst for adventure that continues to this day—a drive to spend time on the sharp edge of life, to take my measure on the rivers, lakes, mountains, cliffs, and wild areas where skill and judgment are more important than luck.

In the 1970s my only role models for being an outdoorswoman were my peers at Outward Bound. I spent more time on the trail than in the library and had no knowledge of the women who had paddled, hiked, climbed, and lived their own lives of adventure years before. But I began to read about early female adventurers and found inspiration in their lives. I searched in particular for women who had satisfied their thirst in the backcountry—hiking mountains, paddling rivers and lakes, climbing cliffs, and venturing far from civilization—women who had tested their bodies and spirits and then returned to their other lives stronger for the experience.

I also looked for women who wrote about their adventures. The way a woman describes her companions and the countryside, how she reacts to hardship, what she includes in the narrative, what she leaves out all provide clues to personality and psyche. I wanted to know how these women felt about being a woman in a "man's world," whom (if anyone) they turned to for support and guidance, and what made some women succeed against all odds. I especially enjoyed the thoughtful, engaging narrations, as well as the epic page-turners.

It was important to learn about these women's lives so I could place their adventures into context. What prompted them to set out for the wilderness? How did their adventures affect their lives back home? Why did they write about their experiences? Did they encourage other women to participate in similar adventures?

This book presents my favorite women of the late 1800s and early 1900s. These women cut through gender expectations of the day and responded to an irresistible draw to adventure. They took risks, polished their skills, and wrote movingly of their experiences. These women, all from the United States or Canada, pursued their dreams in North America or, in one case, South America.

I have only respect for Martha Whitman, who bushwhacked through the White Mountains wearing a long skirt, remained merry and enthusiastic in the face of spruce thickets and short rations, and became a doctor more than a hundred years ago when the medical establishment thought women were too frail and weak-minded to heal the sick.

Pauline Johnson is a woman of my own heart, a canoeist who listened to the song her paddle sang. The daughter of a Mohawk chief, she learned to canoe from her brothers and turned a careful ear to the stories her grandfather told her. When she took to the recital platform as a public performer, she worked resolutely to expose the injustices committed against Native Americans and to reverse the stereotype of Indians as savages. She never called herself a feminist, yet she cared deeply about the plight of Indian women. Johnson's canoe trips may have seemed less adventurous to her than they did to her readers in the 1890s; the rivers, lakes, and woodlands were not alien and threatening but were part of her homeland.

Annie Peck is a curious mixture of struggle and success. Of the women represented here, she alone spoke openly about the difficulties of being a woman in the male world of the outdoors. She had trouble managing her guides; they wouldn't acknowledge her experience, skill, and judgment, and they constantly let her down. Even when she had set the Western Hemisphere altitude record, she found doors closed to her that would have been open to men. She was proud of the fact that she was a single woman and used "Miss" before her name on lecture fliers and invitations to let people know her achievements were her own. She also supported women's suffrage, placing a "Votes for Women" banner on a mountaintop in Peru.

In contrast to Peck, Dora Keen sought the mountains for her own enjoyment and not as a career. She had climbed extensively before reading about an unclimbed peak in Alaska that was "worthy of the hardiest mountaineer." Instead of sending for Swiss guides, she hired locals who could handle rough work and adverse weather. When she failed to reach the summit one year, she went back the next. In conditions that would make modern mountaineers blanch, Keen climbed Mount Blackburn in the Wrangell Range in a small, light, alpine-style expedition in 1912.

Grace Gallatin Seton, who was "born believing in suffrage," was a city person who preferred hot baths to horses but was willing to accompany her husband on trips to study wildlife. On the surface her two books about outdoor life show a woman who is trying to please her wise and all-knowing husband. The subtext, though, reveals a woman who is becoming increasingly more independent on the trail. Seton passed along tips to help other women become more self-sufficient. She campaigned tirelessly for the vote, and she sought out the far corners of the earth for subsequent adventures, going to Egypt, India, China, Southeast Asia, and South America.

I couldn't resist including Elinore Pruitt Stewart because she represents those who by necessity have had to choose more humble—but no less exciting—adventures. Stewart never went to South America or China; she never made a first ascent. Sometimes she barely had enough money to buy paper. She did decide to leave the soot and noise of Denver to homestead in Wyoming (an adventure in itself), and on the rare days when she could get away she lit out with her young daughter on camping trips. Her charming, unpretentious letters to her former employer in Denver caught the public interest in 1913 and 1914, and they still captivate readers today.

Mary Roberts Rinehart had a husband, three children, a highly successful career, and unrelenting guilt about not devoting enough time to any of them. After reporting from the front lines in Europe in 1915, she needed a balm for her soul and found it in a trip (without her family) through the newly opened Glacier Park. This initial adventure led to others. Rinehart found she could assuage her guilt by taking her family with her: she thus satisfied her need for adventure, spent time with her family, and obtained settings and themes for her articles and books.

Mary Jobe was a history teacher at the college level who visited the wild lands of British Columbia and returned again and again to explore, map, and collect ethnographic information. She opened a camp to teach girls how to live in the outdoors. She married Carl Akeley, who was in charge of developing the African Hall at the American Museum of Natural History in New York, and accompanied him on his next trip to Africa. The trip turned out to be his last; Jobe assumed leadership of the expedition when he died and made it her life mission to complete the African Hall.

Marion Randall Parsons called to me through the pages of the *Sierra Club Bulletin*, where she wrote for more than twenty years about her adventures in the mountains. Parsons was indefatigable; she climbed in the Sierras, the Cascades, the Olympics, the Selkirks, the Canadian Rockies, and the Alps. She climbed quietly, never seeking fame, only comradeship and beauty in the outdoors. Her actions speak of her love for the backcountry and its important place in her life. Her writings provide insight into what it was like to be a woman backpacker in the early 1900s.

As I read about these women and their achievements, it became clear that they did not represent a cross-section of women at the time. Whereas in the late 1800s girls customarily had access to elementary and secondary schooling, only an elite few could afford college. Four of the women here—Martha Whitman, Dora Keen, Mary Jobe, and Annie Peck—graduated from college; Jobe and Peck obtained masters degrees. Keen and Jobe attended Bryn Mawr, a women's college outside Philadelphia; women's colleges in the northeastern United States were an important avenue by which women of this time could obtain an education equal to that available to men.

By 1900 about 20 percent of women age sixteen and older earned money outside the home. In the early 1900s most of these women worked on farms, as domestic servants, or in manufacturing. About 8 percent were in professions such as teaching and nursing, and a small percentage held clerical positions or worked in trade.

Several of the women profiled here started out in traditional occupations like teaching, nursing, or domestic work but then moved on to other professions. Martha Whitman supported herself as a teacher for many years before becoming a doctor. Mary Roberts Rinehart was trained in nursing but became one of the most read and highest-paid authors of her day. Elinore Pruitt Stewart worked as a domestic and then became a homesteader. Annie Peck began as a teacher, went back to school and became a college professor, and then turned to a career as a mountaineer, travel writer, and expert on South American affairs. Mary

Jobe taught history at the college level before gaining recognition as an explorer, lecturer, and author.

Other women took a different approach. Dora Keen was involved in civic and volunteer efforts before briefly lecturing about her experiences on Mount Blackburn, settling down as a farmer, and eventually becoming an insurance agent. Pauline Johnson horrified her respectable family by launching a career as a public performer, giving readings of her poetry. Grace Gallatin Seton, a matron of society, was also a book designer, writer, lecturer, and explorer. (Marion Randall Parsons left too little information in her articles to allow us to know what jobs, if any, she held throughout her life.)

Money helped some of these women to satisfy their thirst for adventure, but it was not a prerequisite. Dora Keen's family money allowed her to organize several expeditions to Alaska without having to worry about the cost. Grace Gallatin Seton propelled herself to the farthest reaches of the globe with her family's wealth. And although she had grown up poor, Mary Roberts Rinehart earned enough to take her family around the world many times had she chosen to do so.

Martha Whitman, Pauline Johnson, and Elinore Pruitt Stewart found adventure close to home, so their investment was of time more than money. Annie Peck came from a prosperous family that largely rejected her. She mounted ambitious expeditions and thus spent much of her time between trips raising money; lack of adequate funding doomed several expeditions to South America.

Mary Jobe arranged her life so she could combine vocation and avocation. She taught during the academic year and joined other people's expeditions—and ultimately led her own—during summers. Marriage, work, and a love for the country later took her to Africa. The financial situation of Marion Randall Parsons is somewhat unclear. Her affluent family fell on hard times when Parsons was twenty-two, but she appears to have lived comfortably during her marriage and widowhood.

As a whole, these women were better educated, had more money, and held more professional positions than the average woman at the time. In an era when women were expected to marry and have children, a third of the women here (Martha Whitman, Annie Peck, and Pauline Johnson) did not marry, and two (Dora Keen and Mary Jobe) married only in their mid-forties. Only Mary Roberts Rinehart, Grace Gallatin Seton, and Elinore Pruitt Stewart had children. Three women—Elinore Pruitt Stewart (in her first marriage), Dora Keen, and Grace Gallatin Seton—were divorced.

These women engaged in their adventures at a time when social norms were dramatically different from today. Martha Whitman hiked in a long skirt; Marion Randall Parsons hiked in a shorter one. Grace Gallatin Seton and Mary Roberts Rinehart rode horseback in riding suits that passed as skirts when they were not riding. Annie Peck wore knickerbockers; Dora Keen and Mary Jobe wore pants. This much we know. But these women do not mention what it was like to be the only woman in a group of men when nature called or how they handled their periods, menstrual cramps, and hot flashes on trail. I can only marvel at their apparent adaptability and stoicism.

I still search for adventure. Sometimes I find it writ large, as on a return to the Arctic with women friends when the momentous event was not a desperate rapid but a quiet nighttime visit to our tent by a curious wolf. And sometimes I find it writ small, as when I'm leading out on a stretch of rock that demands intense concentration or paddle around a point and find myself in violent, chaotic waters. I carry with me the images of the women presented here, women who have inspired me and given me insights into being an outdoorswoman. I hope you enjoy their stories as well and will be encouraged to pursue your own adventures.

ACKNOWLEDGMENTS

I am especially indebted to the staff members at the Maine State Library, Augusta, Maine, who were unfailingly helpful and cheerful. Both attributes count for a lot during the long course of researching a manuscript.

I would also like to acknowledge the valuable assistance of the following individuals and institutions: Christine Haberl, the Alpine Club of Canada; Bangor Public Library, Bangor, Maine; Bancroft Library, University of California, Berkeley; Emily Beattie, Director of Technical Services, Boston University School of Medicine; Lorett Treese, Archivist, Bryn Mawr Archives, Bryn Mawr College, Bryn Mawr, Pennsylvania; Cary Memorial Library, Lexington, Massachusetts; Jim Davidson; Hawthorne-Longfellow Library, Bowdoin College, Brunswick, Maine; Miller Library, Colby College, Waterville, Maine; Helen Keith, Curator, Mystic River Historical Society, Inc., Mystic, Connecticut; Portland Public Library, Portland, Maine; Janice Kruger, Administrator, Society of Women Geographers, Washington, D.C.; Smith College Archives, Northampton, Massachusetts; Ann B. Gray, Director, Stonington Library, Stonington, Connecticut; Gwyneth Hoyle, Librarian Emeritus, Trent University, Peterborough, Ontario; Wendy Godley, Special Collections Division, Vancouver Public Library, Vancouver, British Columbia.

Particular thanks go to my editor, Marykay Cicio, for her thoughtful guidance and to Cheryl Carnahan for her careful editing. I am grateful to Sheila McDonald, Mary McClintock, Audrey Ingersol, and Meneely Townsend for their insightful comments on the manuscript. Of course, any errors are my own.

Thanks to all of the women with whom I have shared adventure in the backcountry. Beth Barker, Sue Minors, Carol Gentry Gray, Jean Hoekwater, Ruthie Rhode, Anne Dellenbaugh, Sandy Neily, Mellen Shea, Nancy Burns, Kathy Nilsen, Pat Bergman, Jean Faloon, Marty Moscrip,

Nancy Pike, Annie Getchell, and Kate McClain are only a few of my many wonderful trail companions over the years. Although I did more planning than paddling with the founding and early board members of Women Outdoors, our discussions of what it means to be professional outdoorswomen and how to teach outdoor leadership skills to women were an important part of my growth.

A special thanks goes to Ben Townsend—my husband, friend, enduring supporter, and trusted outdoor partner—for understanding my need for adventure and for helping me to fulfill it.

1

ENCOURAGING LADIES TO CAMP

Martha Whitman

(1840–1884)

> *For the first time I fully realized our situation. Night was coming on; we could hardly reach the woods before darkness would be upon us; the only implement we had for building a shelter was the knife I wore in my belt; our stock of matches had become wet, and dry wood was not to be found.*

There was nothing in Martha Whitman's early life to suggest that she would become an outdoorswoman, let alone a doctor. At the time she was born women were either schoolteachers, as Martha was for many years, or housewives. Because it was extremely difficult for women to surmount the prejudice that kept them from climbing mountains, it was unusual to find women who enjoyed and pursued outdoor adventure.

Mount Washington.

In their book *Forest and Crag* (1989), Laura and Guy Waterman characterize the years between 1820 and 1870 in the northeastern United States as an era when women had to overcome barriers of attitudes. "It was, to put it mildly, not an age when women either expected or were expected to show athletic vigor or an adventurous bent." But from 1870 to 1910 "walking clubs" began to form, and women in the Catskills, Adirondacks, White Mountains, and other areas had a new, if limited, opportunity to get outdoors.

Martha Whitman's life straddled these two eras, and she lived the transition. Her early experiences in the outdoors convinced her that women belonged there as much as men. She believed women could learn to do all the work needed to camp comfortably and safely in the wild, including choosing a campsite and pitching a tent, and she tried to persuade other women to give camping a try.

"I desire to let [women] know that they may, if they will, do almost the same mountain work as men, may visit those delightful spots which have hitherto been but a name to them, may fish in streams sufficiently remote from civilization to contain trout more than two or three inches long, may enjoy views not down in the Guide Book even, and in this way may visit places usually regarded as inaccessible." She wasn't concerned with women who feared muddying their shoes or having their faces browned by the sun—they were better off in hotels. She reached out to women "who fear only from inexperience."

Whitman began setting an independent course when she became interested in camping. She had been going on outings with the Lexington Botanical Club—a group of "four ladies and two gentlemen"—staying in hotels and exploring the White Mountains of New Hampshire. As the club's name indicates, its members were interested in botany, an acceptable way to see new countryside during the Victorian age.

Whether the primary focus was the study of botany or the places their studies took them, club members were clearly inspired by their life out-of-doors. "We loved the mountains, every rock and rill, every ravine and ridge, but we loved them as we first saw them, when little of fashion or sham penetrated so far." As more and more people headed to the mountains, the charm disappeared. The friends decided to venture farther into the mountains to reach "less frequented places" and avoid those "who go only to say they have been." That's when they decided to take up camping.

In their first excursion the friends camped for three weeks near Conway, New Hampshire, at the southern end of the White Mountains. Their experiment was so successful, even with imperfect equipment, that they decided to continue. "We have every year since shunned the hotels, and, to a great extent, the frequented places, and set up our housekeeping wherever we desired."

Sometimes they rode horses, stopping for one or several nights depending on what the area offered. "At other times we have been conveyed far into the wilderness, and have trusted to fortune to get out again. . . . And thus in one way or another we have camped throughout the White and Franconia Mountains, and beyond, through the Grafton Notch to Lake Umbagog, and through the Dixville Range to the sources of the Connecticut." The Lexington Botanical Club had effectively covered much of New Hampshire and some of Maine.

These camping trips helped Whitman to understand and lay bare the fears that prevented women from experiencing the joys of camping in the 1870s. "Women who talk with us about camp, and who know nothing about it, seem to think it must be a life of hardship, and ask us if we are comfortable in a tent. 'What do you have to eat?' 'How do you lay your table?' 'Are you not afraid of insects?' 'Are you much annoyed by bears?' and 'Don't you take cold?'"

She responded to such queries by describing the ease and benefits of wilderness camping. She lauded the virtues of a hemlock bed and described how to make one: Lay down a rubber blanket, carefully arrange the hemlock boughs, and place wool blankets on top. Make a pillow of more boughs or use a piece of clothing stuffed into a cambric bag. Although the first night out there was generally little sleep on account of "considerable growling and many poor jokes," thereafter the "real luxury of sleep begins—a luxury of rest and comfort, the senses soothed with the aroma of hemlock, and lulled by the rippling of a mountain stream—a sleep that brings strength for the hardest climbs."

As for wild animals and insects, a person could see as many in a farm field as on a camping trip. "Indeed our longing has seldom been gratified by finding even the track of a bear." Insects were "easily managed." In camp, black flies and mosquitoes were dealt with by the judicious use of netting around the tent walls and door, as well as a smoky fire. Sometimes a veil of netting gathered at the shoulders was necessary when tramping in the evening. Midges, which can go through netting, were another matter entirely. Martha advised, "The only way to avoid them is not to go where they are. Don't go into the mountains until they are gone." She counseled that midges decrease in July and vanish by August.

What exactly did "roughing it" mean to Whitman? She explained: "For a trip to last two or three days, when light luggage only can be taken, one can do very well with a towel and a comb, hard tack and oatmeal, and a simple shelter of canvas or bark." But in most cases the "decencies of life" were entirely compatible "with real enjoyment of nature in her wilder forms. . . . We believe in having as many conveniences as possible, even luxuries, if one can afford it."

In an era when societal mores strictly dictated women's dress, Whitman was so bold as to advocate that when women ventured into the mountains they wear a loose-fitting "short" skirt that came to the top of the boots. A longer skirt could be carried along for appearing in public. Although her recommendation hardly seems daring by today's standards, in her day it was startling indeed. As late as 1896, Cornelia "Fly Rod" Crosby—a fishing guide and writer from Maine—created a scandal when she appeared at the Second Annual Sportsman's Show in New York in a lady's hunting outfit, the hem of which was a shocking 7 inches off the floor.

Whitman recommended that a woman camper have two complete suits of clothing, two pairs of boots, and an ample supply of thick stockings. Wool flannel was the best fabric for dresses because it was strong and easily cleaned; it was cool during the heat of the day but kept out the chill in evenings and during rainy weather. A woman should also take gloves, a shade hat, rubber boots, and a "waterproof" to protect her from rain.

Every camper knows food can make or break a trip. Food was important, and Whitman extolled it. Because fresh eggs and milk were generally available in outlying areas, the possibilities were legion. "Who would not be satisfied with a breakfast like this: coffee, for everybody drinks coffee in camp; oatmeal mush, with icy cold cream; potatoes baked to a turn and taken directly from the ashes to your plate, or fried, crisp and thin, rivalling even Revere chips; brook trout, caught an hour before, or breakfast bacon in thin crisp slices, just a delicate shade of brown, with fresh eggs in any style; golden Johnny cake smoking from the oven, followed by rice fritters served with bread, sweet butter and maple syrup." When Whitman and her group first camped, they rigged an umbrella over the fire so they could bake beans and boil apple pudding on rainy days. Subsequently, they honed their skills in the camp kitchen. "In these days of prepared fruits, meats and vegetables it is not difficult to have supplies of almost everything desired, even in the wilderness."

Whitman does not say exactly when she began going on outings with the Lexington Club, but she must have been old enough to go without a chaperon. In other words, she must already have been a "spinster," a woman past marriageable age—perhaps 30 years old. At any rate, she had spent considerable time in the backcountry before she joined the Appalachian Mountain Club (AMC) in 1876, the year following its organization.

Whitman gave a presentation to the membership in early 1877 about an ill-fated trip to Mount Washington (see "A Climb Through Tuckerman's Ravine," following). She and her friends had been camping in the mountains for several weeks, choosing a base camp and exploring the area until moving on. They reached a valley east of Mount

Washington by mid-August, pitching their tents along the Peabody River. One day they set off down Notch Road, visiting Thompson's Falls, Crystal Cascade, and Glen Ellis Falls on the Ellis River. They headed back to Crystal Cascade, arriving just past noon. So far, they had hiked about 5 miles.

One of Whitman's companions suggested following the stream, so they could hike up the side of Washington and into Tuckerman Ravine to examine the Snow Arch, which forms as meltwater flows under the snowfield and eats away the snow from below. Because of the summer heat Whitman and her companion left their heavy clothing with their friends and started for the ravine at 2 P.M., promising to return to camp at dark.

With good conditions their estimate would not have been far off. The trip from Crystal Cascade to the Snow Arch is a little over 2 miles. Allowing four hours to get there and another three hours to return, they would have showed up in camp at 9 P.M. But Whitman and her companion became lost below the Snow Arch and got caught in a sudden storm.

Throughout their struggle in the hours that followed, they were haunted by the memory of Lizzie Bourne, who had died on the same mountain. On September 15, 1855, Lizzie had joined her uncle and cousin on a sortie up the Crawford bridle path. They got a late start, and by nightfall they were buffeted by high winds and got wet to the skin. They struggled on as far as they could but finally collapsed and waited for dawn. Lizzie, just twenty-three years old, died in the dark on Washington. Ironically, the little group lay only 600 feet from the Summit House, where a warm fire, food, and dry clothes awaited.

Martha Whitman's narration of her experience on Washington provides a classic description of what can go wrong in the mountains. It is easy to be unprepared; the weather can change dramatically, and nightfall can make escape more difficult. Whitman was not the first person—or the last—to be lured up Washington on a sunny afternoon without extra clothing, a "waterproof," and food. The mountain has some of the worst weather in North America, and more than one hundred people have died on its slopes.

Whitman regularly attended AMC field meetings and hiked in New Hampshire throughout the early 1880s. When another AMC member organized a seven-day bushwhacking trip through the Twin Mountain Range in 1882, he invited Whitman along. Throughout the punishing ordeal she was "merry and enthusiastic." Marion Pychowska, an AMC member who also hiked extensively, described Whitman as "evidently very independent, but ladylike and unassuming. I think she is the most thoroughly good lady mountaineer I have ever seen, short and stout and therefore somewhat scant of breath, but energetic and untiring. She seems to go through exposure, fatigue and camp food with unimpaired digestion."

By the time Martha Whitman turned her sights toward becoming a doctor, she knew she was strong, could endure fatigue and loss of sleep, and could handle exposure to weather at all hours of the day or night. She was confident of her abilities and was used to challenging herself, so she was well equipped to face the prejudices against women, as illustrated in an excerpt from the *Boston Medical and Surgical Journal*: "In the physical condition of women, also, we find much in support of our views. The weakness of her bodily organization renders her less fit to undergo the incessant fatigue, the loss of sleep, the exposure to weather at all hours of the day and night, which are the lot of the active medical practitioner."

Why should she listen to frowning men who said no when she had already done many things women weren't supposed to do? Martha Whitman was a self-made woman with a clear identity of self. She applied to the medical school at Boston University, a rigorous three-year program, and received a Doctor of Medicine degree in 1884.

Whitman signed on as resident physician in a Boston institution. But later in 1884 she met a challenge strength of character alone could not overcome. She may have caught typhoid fever from a patient with the disease, or she could have gotten it from infected milk or water in those times of poor sanitation. Whatever the cause, she died from typhoid fever shortly before Christmas. At their next meeting her AMC friends mourned the passing of an avid hiker and a beloved companion.

A Climb Through Tuckerman's Ravine

The grandeur of Glen Ellis, with its unbroken leap, held us entranced so long that it was past noon when we found ourselves back at Crystal Cascade.

While discussing our lunch on the precipice above, just out of reach of the guide book tourist, one of the gentlemen of our little party, who had often been our leader in exploration, challenged us to follow up the stream to the snow arches in Tuckerman's Ravine. I had long desired to explore this region, and, feeling great confidence in his powers as well as my own for the work, without hesitation announced my readiness to start upon the instant. The rest not feeling inclined to join, we left our heavy wraps with them to be taken back to camp, and divested ourselves of all but the most necessary luggage, which little we carried slung to our belts.

At a little past two o'clock we started, promising to be back in camp at dark with true mountain appetites for a hot supper.

As has been stated at former meetings of the club, the old path is considerably overgrown, and in many places the blazes are obscure, but we rambled leisurely along, every step a revelation of beauty such as is only seen in the deep recesses of the unbroken forest. Rank beds of fern covered with a veil of loveliness the scars left by trees uprooted by the winter's storms; the beautiful Linnaea in many places bordered the path; orchids, both old friends and new, seemed to spring up in every direction luring us from our way in our eager search for floral treasures; beds of starry Oxalis tempted us to stop and revel in their beauty, while our indolence was awakened by the dainty upholstery of soft green mosses on huge old logs. But amid all these temptations we did not lose sight of our object. It was a constant climb, but so filled with delight, so brimming with invigoration and excitement, that we heeded not the work or the passing hour.

Neither did we heed what afterward proved a serious matter for us.

As we came out of the forest upon the cleared space just above Hermit Lake, we observed for the first time that the sky had become clouded and a dense blackness was fast settling down upon the ravine. The solitude of the place was awe-inspiring, the walls of the ravine rising so steep in front and on either side, the unbroken forest behind, and below us a lake whose black stillness seemed weird and dreadful. No wind seemed to ruffle its inky surface though the clouds were scudding rapidly over our heads. But we did not tarry long, neither was there a word said about turning back. We were accustomed to accomplish whatever we attempted and the casual glimpses of the snow beyond, apparently so near, but which we found so far, encouraged us on.

We rapidly passed through the low growth of wood just beyond the lake, reached the alders and were soon utterly lost. To those who have never traveled that road it is impossible to convey any definite idea of its horrors; added to the natural difficulties of the way, we had hardly struck into the alders when the clouds shut in around us, drenching us to the skin and weighing down the bushes so as to obliterate all traces of previous footsteps.

We floundered about wildly, first on one side, then on the other, the wet alders lashing us with icy boughs as if resenting our efforts to force a passage.

We were finally compelled to take to the middle of the stream. At first we jumped from rock to rock trying to keep our feet from the waters fresh from beds of ice. But we soon plunged boldly in, wading as we might, knee deep and sometimes deeper. Those who are familiar with that stream—or those streams, for it constantly divides—remember that it is filled with boulders, some of them completely blocking the way. It is not pleasant to boost another up a slippery rock in the face of an ice-cold cascade, but this I frequently did and was pulled up afterward, having but one boast to make for my part of the work, that in no case did I require assistance where I had not also to give it.

Out of the alders the snow arches seem close at hand, but benumbed with cold, weighed down with wet clothes, and with clouds freighted with rain dashing in your face, the scramble over the rocks is neither easy nor agreeable. I fear our course from Hermit Lake to the arches could hardly be called a pleasure walk, neither can we boast of our walking time, but at last we accomplished it and stood sheltered beneath a roof of ice and snow.

Under some circumstances it might have seemed a shelter in fairy land, and we should have lingered long, as we have since done, in examining its wonders. Above, the vaulted roof studded with a million projecting points, from each of which ran a tiny stream or hung a glistening drop; beneath, the streams dancing over the rocks, and the whole interior lighted by that strange greenish light which penetrates the roof; before the entrance, within a radius of a hundred yards, a fine procession of flowers, from the curiously folded *Veratrum* just piercing the frozen ground at the edge of the ice, to the goldenrod of late summer.

But now it seemed rather an abode of demons. The Thousand Streams had become foaming torrents and rushed down the precipice above us and through the ice caverns with a deafening roar. The winds howled, the clouds thickened and thickened as the storm every moment increased, and the black walls of the ravine seemed to be shutting us in closer and closer.

For the first time I fully realized our situation. Night was coming on, we could hardly reach the woods before darkness would be upon us, the only implement we had for building a shelter was the knife I wore in my belt, our stock of matches had become wet and dry wood was not to be found. Our provisions consisted of two hard crackers and a very small pocket-flask, with not more than a spoonful of brandy, and to increase the danger we were wet to the skin and shaking with cold. All this passed rapidly through my mind, but what was in the mind of my companion I knew not, for little had been said during the last hour and I would not by a question indicate to him that I had the slightest anxiety. At last he broke the silence. "To return is impossible; our only hope is to reach the top. Are you equal to it?" With no conception of the further difficulties before us, but reading the necessity from the tone and look of my companion, I answered, "I think I am," and without delay we started.

We knew nothing of the path from the ravine to the top and had no time to explore. All this time the clouds had been falling lower and lower, covering the tops of the cliffs and even obscuring their sides. But as we stood facing down the ravine we discovered on our left what seemed to be the bed of a spring torrent or the track of a slide. We selected this for our attempt. Up, up we went, clinging to twigs of spruce and willow, or when those failed us to the very grass and ferns; often on our hands and knees, sometimes pushing and pulling each other in turn; carefully, for every step sent loosened stones bounding down, warning us by the sound how far a misstep might send us; often finding our way blocked by some steep cliff or huge rock whose vertical face offered us no hold for foot or hand, then a climb around to one side and then the other to find a way, but always up, till, at last, a climb, which I cannot now look back upon without a shudder and which later examination convinces me we never could have accomplished had not our haste prevented our looking back and the darkness obscured the danger of the way, was ended.

But our perils were not yet over. As soon as we were above the protecting walls of the ravine the storm struck us with its full force, compelling us to cling to each other for support. Night was hard upon us and the clouds so dense we could hardly see a dozen rods ahead.

There was no time to be lost, and scarcely stopping to take breath we turned in what we supposed to be the direction of the carriage road. Almost immediately we were plunged into that dense sea of scrub which lies between the road and the ravine on the northeasterly side. We floundered helplessly, the wind driving us and the scrub with its briarean arms dragging us in. At last we escaped and hastily retraced our steps to the edge of the ravine. Again we started—this time following around the head of the ravine and striking off in a northwesterly direction, as nearly as we could guess, for the old Crawford bridle path, with which we were somewhat familiar, having passed over it but a few days before.

Let me say in passing that I speak of directions and localities from information afterward gained; at the time I had no idea of the direction of the summit, the road, or the path, and knew not the intention of my companion, for little was said; he took the lead and I followed blindly.

Occasionally fierce gusts laden with sleet would strike us, compelling us to crouch and cling to the very rocks.

Bareheaded and with skirts close reefed, on we went, not daring to stop a moment in our chilled condition, knowing the necessity of speed, yet realizing the dangers of bewilderment and that a single misstep on those icy rocks might end in disaster, hardly daring to hope we were steering in the right direction, when suddenly, as our courage was at its utmost tension, and our helplessness in the face of the furious elements, and our loneliness on that mountain waste more and more drear in the gathering blackness, had become almost appalling, the clouds parted for a moment, revealing directly ahead of us the unmistakable outline of the summit of Mount Monroe.

With a cheery "We are all right," on we went with renewed courage, changing our course as much as we dared toward the summit but with slower and more careful steps in the increasing darkness until at last we came to a ridge of stones apparently thrown up by human hands, over which we stumbled and found ourselves in the bridle path. We were not a moment too soon, for our strength was nearly exhausted, and it was now so dark we could hardly distinguish each other's faces.

For the first time I knew where we were, and though remembering the difficulties yet before us felt that we were safe. A sigh of relief was the only outward expression of feeling from a heart too grateful for speech.

Many of you are familiar with that last mile up the cone, and will appreciate the difficulties of traveling it by night in the blackness of a furious storm. How we did it I cannot tell. I only remember that we felt every step of the way—sometimes on foot, often on hands and knees—and that somehow we reached the old corral, the end of the bridle path. Here sheltered slightly from the force of the storm we rested for a moment and I was at last allowed the spoonful of brandy which to this time had remained untouched in our flask—my companion dryly remarking that Lizzie Bourne perished even nearer the summit than we were. We soon left the corral and slowly dragged ourselves over those huge boulders which surround the immediate summit, with nothing to guide us save the sense of feeling and the knowledge that we must go up.

So thick was the night that we struck the platform which surrounds the house before we discerned a gleam of light. We hesitated a moment with a realizing sense of our ludicrous appearance, but finally opened the door and stood—hatless, with remnants only of shoes, stockings, and skirts, before the wondering crowd which surrounded the blazing fire.

Our kind host came at once to our relief, furnished us with dry clothes, hot food and drinks; and after a telegram had relieved our anxious friends and stopped a party of men from the Glen House who had started out with guides and lanterns to search for us, we were soon oblivious of our perils in that slumber which only comes to mountain climbers.

Pauline Johnson in 1892, wearing her first Indian costume for recitals.

2

THE SONG MY PADDLE SINGS
E. Pauline Johnson
Tekahionwake
(1862–1913)

We ran our first rapids, too, that day.
They were glorious. Oh! those
indescribably splendid rapids that throng
the far inland rivers of Canada, that
swirl, scurry and scamper among their
stones, whose voices whisper along velvet
shores, then break into rollicking
laughter as they dash on their immovable
boulders and split into a million bubbles
that fall and float away like countless
unset pearls.

The call of quiet, wild places came early to Pauline
Johnson, and it came rather naturally. Her father was George

Henry Martin Johnson, a Mohawk who was chief of the Six Nations, a confederation of Iroquois tribes that included the Mohawk. Her mother was Emily Howells, a British woman who—much to her family's dismay—married an Indian. The cultural influences of both sides of the family provided the shape and force of Johnson's life.

Johnson was raised at Chiefswood, a beautiful colonial home on the shore of the Grand River near Brantford, Ontario. A constant flow of Native American, Canadian, and English dignitaries visited Chief Johnson, providing his daughter and her three siblings with an unusual and stimulating education in the issues of the day. Both parents passed on a love of reading that, in turn, fostered an interest in writing.

Johnson also spent long hours with her grandfather, Smoke Johnson (Tekahionwake), a great warrior and orator who taught her Mohawk culture and history. From her brothers she learned to canoe, snowshoe, and use a bow and arrow, all of which became second nature to her. Throughout her life she found herself drawn to water.

After years of home schooling and just two years of formal education, Johnson returned to Chiefswood at age sixteen and settled into a pleasant life in which she was at leisure to read, write, and entertain herself. She and her friends camped at Muskoka Lake near Georgian Bay, paddling and idling away the sunny hours. The lake became one of Johnson's favorite places, and she later returned to it in poetry when she could not go there in person.

Johnson's writings about this time in her life reflect how comfortable she was in the outdoors, on the river, and in a canoe. In fact, Johnson paddled her own canoe, the *Wildcat*, which she helped design. On one trip to an unnamed river in northern Ontario, she and her female friend Puck braved the challenges of a wilderness river without the aid of male muscle. "Beauless and bold," they held up well under the rigors of the 80-mile trip, which included stiff head winds, frothy rapids, and a calamitous thunderstorm (see "Ripples and Paddle Plashes: A Canoe Story," following).

On another trip she took the stern of the *Wildcat* with her friend

Joe in the bow. Joe was a dreamer who could neither fry a fish nor steer a canoe. It was Johnson who set the sail on a breezy day, chose the course through the rapids, and kept the boat out of trouble. Joe was happy to place all responsibility in Johnson's skillful hands.

Johnson enjoyed a glorious youth at Chiefswood and on her summer retreats. As she became a young woman, she—like most women of her age—was simply biding time until she got married. But her carefree life ended with the death of her father when she was twenty-three. Johnson's mother could not maintain Chiefswood financially, and the family moved into the town of Brantford. Johnson could no longer afford to while away the hours. She, like Mary Roberts Rinehart, needed to support herself in an era when respectable women did not work and few women had marketable skills. This transition marked the end of Johnson's easy access to the wild lands she loved, but she returned to the familiar comfort of her canoe and the soulful cadence of paddle meeting water whenever she could.

Johnson's interest lay in poetry. Her first verse was published a year after her father's death. In recognition of her Mohawk heritage she added her grandfather's name, Tekahionwake, to her own in 1886. In 1889 two of her poems appeared in an anthology, *Songs of the Great Dominion*. She received encouragement from several poets, including John Greenleaf Whittier. But poetry brought in no money, so she looked for other opportunities.

Johnson's big break came in January 1892, when she and other writers were invited to read their verse at a recital in Toronto. The evening dragged along until Johnson took the stage. "Thrilling was the effect, dramatic the appeal of this dark-hued girl who seemed to personify her race. It was the Indian who spoke, the Indian woman, as with intense passion she voiced the cry of her kind," wrote Frank Yeigh, who listened with particular attention. The audience was stunned into silence, then slowly everyone began applauding in waves. "Rarely does an audience so rapidly change its mood, and rarely does a reciter so capture her hearers," continued Yeigh. Yeigh asked Johnson if he could serve as her manager, and at age thirty she began a career as a dramatic reciter.

Johnson won her mother's reluctant approval to tour as a recitalist by emphasizing that the money would be used to further her career as a poet. Being a poet was acceptable, but being a recitalist was close to being an actress. In Emily Howells Johnson's world no woman of decent upbringing became an actress, as actresses had loose morals and bad reputations.

One month after the recital Johnson drew inspiration from her days in the *Wildcat* and wrote the poem that became her most famous. In "The Song My Paddle Sings" she tells of the freedom, beauty, and danger she finds with her cherished companions—canoe and paddle— on a flowing, dancing river. Although contemporary readers may find the verses stilted, audiences in the 1890s were entranced by Johnson's celebration of the natural world and the canoeist's place in it.

> August is laughing across the sky,
> Laughing while paddle, canoe and I,
>   Drift, drift,
> Where the hills uplift
> On either side of the current swift.
>
> The river rolls in its rocky bed;
> My paddle is plying the way ahead;
>   Dip, dip
> While the waters flip
> In foam as over their breast we slip.
>
> And oh, the river runs swifter now;
> The eddies circle about my bow.
>   Swirl, swirl!
> How the rapids curl
> In many a dangerous pool awhirl!

Be strong, O paddle! be brave, canoe!
The reckless waves you must plunge
    into.
   Reel, reel.
On your trembling keel,
But never a fear my craft will feel.

We've raced the rapid, we're far ahead!
The river slips through its silent bed.
   Sway, sway,
As the bubbles spray
And fall in tinkling tunes away.

And up on the hills against the sky,
A fir tree rocking its lullaby,
   Swings, swings,
Its emerald wings,
Swelling the song that my paddle sings.

With Yeigh's help Johnson's first recital led to numerous others in eastern Canada, where she was close enough to the Grand River to grab the *Wildcat* and her paddle when she needed to renew her spirit. She also attended canoe club meets, where her experience was widely acknowledged. If she had chosen to compete, she could have been a highly ranked canoeist and possibly the top woman paddler in North America. As it was, she attended these gatherings in eastern Canada and the United States simply to share her love of the activity.

Naturalist Ernest Thompson Seton later wrote in the introduction to Johnson's book *The Shagganappi* that she was "at home equally in the salons of the rich and learned or in the stern of the birch canoe, where, with paddle poised she was in absolute and fearless control, watching, warring and winning against the grim rocks that grinned out of the white rapids to tear the frail craft and mangle its daring rider." Seton's praise is noteworthy, although his choice of metaphor is misleading, for Johnson regarded her accomplishments not as a victory in a war with the natural world but as a means of earning her place in that world. Wilderness was her heritage and her refuge; wilderness accepted her on her own terms. Plying her paddle allowed her to rest and refresh her spirit.

In just two years, between 1892 and 1894, Pauline gave 125 recitals in 50 locations in eastern Canada. She was acclaimed by audiences, but she wanted to be acclaimed by the literati as well. She saved her earnings to help her meet her next goal: to publish a book of her poems. Only a publisher in England or the United States would bring sufficient prestige, so Johnson turned to her mother's homeland to seek recognition.

Johnson went to England in 1894 with a stack of letters of introduction that allowed her access to wealthy and powerful patrons. British society members eager to see and hear the voice of a vanishing culture invited her to perform in their drawing rooms, where she wore a buckskin dress and recited what she called her Indian poems, poems like "A Cry from an Indian Wife" and "As Red Men Die." Her trip was a resounding success. Not only did she mingle with distinguished writers and critics, but she gained the attention of a highly regarded London publisher. Her first collection of poetry, *White Wampum*, received the critical acclaim she coveted.

Johnson was thirty-three when she returned from England, and for the next fifteen years she toured Canada, the United States, and England, performing in large cities as well as remote whistle-stops. She continued to compose romantic verse and occasionally wrote feature articles and stories about Mohawk life. Johnson cared deeply about how Indians—particularly Indian women—were perceived, and many of her poems and stories featured Native American women. She once remarked, "Never let anyone call me a white woman. There are those who think they pay me a compliment in saying that I am just like a white woman. My aim, my joy, my pride is to sing the glories of my own people."

During this time Johnson was beset by the combined stress of earning a living, establishing herself as a Native American poet, and keeping up with a demanding schedule. Her time with the *Wildcat* was limited. A friend from later years observed, however, that "whenever [Johnson] felt bruised by the pressures of life she would always try to escape to a patch of open water and a canoe."

The fact that Johnson sang the glories of her own people in an era when many still considered Indians to be savages is a testament to her vibrant personality and force of character. It is important to remember that Johnson began performing as a dramatic reciter in 1892, just sixteen years after Crazy Horse and other warriors had defeated Custer at the Little Big Horn in 1876 and only two years after U.S. soldiers had massacred Indians at Wounded Knee in 1890. Although Johnson thrilled some audiences with her Indian poems, she was not spared the painful prejudice and rejection that indigenous populations suffered at the time. Johnson's calling placed her in a delicate position. Audiences attended her performances because she was the Mohawk "princess," but at the same time she was an Indian, a group held in low esteem.

In 1898 Johnson became engaged to marry George Drayton, an inspector at the Western Loan and Savings Company in Winnipeg. The marriage promised a return to a simpler life and a security she had not known since her father died. Two years passed before the nagging objections of Drayton's family (that Johnson had appeared on stage and therefore her reputation was suspect) finally prompted him to break the engagement.

Coupled with her mother's death a short time before, the breakup left Johnson bereft. She was orphaned and abandoned, and her sorrow seeped into her writing. As one friend observed, "The defeat of love runs like a grey thread through much of Miss Johnson's verse," including these lines from "The Prodigal":

Ah, me! My paddle failed me in the
steering across love's shoreless sea.

Even in the realm of love, Johnson returned to her comforting paddle. Canoeing was not just a balm to her soul; it was a metaphor for her life.

Johnson's second book of poems, *Canadian Born*, was published in 1903 but was not as well received as her first. The relentless demands of travel sapped Johnson's energy, and the endless performances meant she needed to write continually. She had neither time nor energy to satisfy her calling as a poet. By 1909 she had grown weary of life on the road. She decided to give up touring and support herself solely by writing.

Johnson settled in Vancouver. Joe Capilano, a Squamish chief whom she had befriended on a trip to England, lived there, and on a previous visit he had given her a canoe to use as long as she wished. At that time she had stayed for a month, happily paddling in Burrand Inlet and English Bay. The permanent move to Vancouver was thus in some ways a homecoming.

Johnson was content in her new life, writing articles for magazines and newspapers and developing a circle of friends. But she had ignored for too long a growing lump in her breast, and when she finally consulted a doctor it was too late to curtail the cancer. By late 1911 the opiates she took for pain left her unable to write. Johnson faced death with aplomb, and her feelings about it were singular:

> When we are born into a world of sorrow everyone rejoices; but when we die and go to the happy hunting grounds everyone mourns. Well, I don't want even my best friends to mourn for me. If now and again the people of Canada read some line of my work, which brings home to them the love I have for this great country of mine, then they may remember me as having done my best to share with them something that the Great Tyee had given to me.

Johnson's loyal friends in Vancouver rallied to her aid. When her money ran low, they raised funds to publish collections of her articles, stories, and poems and thus provide her with a trust. She died on March

7, 1913, and her ashes were buried in Stanley Park, a beautiful waterside preserve in Vancouver. L. W. Makovski, a writer for the *Vancouver Province,* included a telling description of her in the newspaper's eulogy: "In spite of her English mother she was an Indian to the core. The trail and the forest, the mountains and the rivers were her home. Four walls could never imprison her great spirit."

Ripples and Paddle Plashes: A Canoe Story

"She's come!" I exclaimed, the instant Puck's aunt opened the door to me.

"Who has come?" queried that lady, with rebuking dignity.

"The *Wildcat,*" I ejaculated.

"And who is the *Wildcat?*" she asked, with increased stateliness.

"My canoe!" Then she gave a comprehensive "oh," smiled sympathetically, and called: "Puck, the *Wildcat* has come!" (I do wish Puck's aunt would not speak so ambiguously sometimes.)

Downstairs bounded my canoeing crony, her tam o'shanter in one hand, her tan shoes in the other, and without even saying good morning to her long-suffering hostess we dashed off to the boat house that we had haunted every day for a week in hopes that each train would bring the little craft wherein we were destined to spend so many happy days.

Oh! but it was a beauty—not a court beauty, all varnished and polished and nickel plated, with Brussels matting and velvet cushions, like some of those on the racks about us, but a sturdy little craft, painted gray inside and out, with the name on the bow in black and gold lettering. It was the regulation 16-foot basswood cruiser, built on the new model, with the high-sweeping, rough-water bows that suggest so strongly the birch bark. The decks were ash, slightly stained and varnished, and a brass keel ran the entire length. I had a great quarrel with the builder over that keel; he said it only increased the weight and was old-fashioned, but I was obstinate, and many times afterward I had reason to be glad that I was so, for when we scraped stony shoals and sheered off boulders my craft was comparatively unharmed, while the rest of the party bemoaned the scratched and ragged condition of their boat bottoms. Well, that morning we ran the *Wildcat* out for a test paddle. She trimmed beautifully with Puck in the bow; light, swift and taut, nothing could have been more satisfactory.

We had talked all winter of this cruise, wherein we two girls were to "break the record" and paddle 80 miles without the aid of masculine muscle. Our party consisted of four canoe loads. The chaperons in one, the other two manned at the stern and girled at the bow. Then Puck and I, beauless and bold, in spite of the chaperon's long hesitation and tardy consent to our undertaking.

"You'll be sure to get drowned," she said.

"You'll be sure to get nothing of the kind," said her husband, who knew my river record, and snorted in derision at the idea of an upset. He swore many times that I had never upset a canoe in my life, which for a wonder was true, because generally when he swore anything it was but his way of emphasizing a falsehood. As for Puck—well, she is a little English girl on her first visit to Canada, a girl with all the grit and daring of a true Briton. She had never been in a canoe in her life until a month before we started on that cruise, but she paddled like a native, steered like an arrow and had learned every trick of launching, breaching and portaging as well as the best of us.

After announcing to the cruising party that the *Wildcat*

had come at last, we spent two days fixing up our last year's flannels, getting blankets, cushions and hampers, borrowing tents, mending sails and collecting together the hundred things that are included in that comprehensive term, "camping kit."

Then came a journey of 60 miles by rail to a village away up in northern Ontario, where the eight tired, hot and dust-begrimed people made for the ramshackle old hotel and clamored for tea, wash bowls and towels, after which we all turned in to enjoy the last civilized bed we were to dream upon for a week.

It was Puck who awakened me the next morning, though there was not much of her in the room, just a pair of heels and a bit of skirt. The rest of her was hanging out of the window, uttering adjectives of ecstatic delight and calling me to "come and look." I went. Ye gods! what a picture it was we saw from that scrimpy little hotel window.

Dawn—gray and daffodil in the east, pearl and ebony in the west, with a purple sky, in which a thousand stars were bleaching, dwindling, disappearing with every second over a wide, rugged landscape that circled a patch of black water lying in deadly stillness a stone's throw distant.

We "ohd" about it for five minutes, then Norton banged at the door (Norton is fiendishly prosaic) and told us to "Get your ears back now, girls, and get a gait on you." We scrambled about in the half light and got dressed, joined the others at breakfast, and just as the sun looked over the cedar tops we all pushed off from the shore.

The landlord, three teamsters, six lumbermen and eleven village sightseers "hurrahed" us off, and one voice raised slightly higher than its fellows announced that "them two little gals is mighty plucky." The four canoes shot out across the lake in Indian file. Mr. and Mrs. Norton, young

E. PAULINE JOHNSON

and genial, with the honeymoon only two years behind them, led. Then came Puck's English cousin, Hampstead (whom I had taught to paddle and was awfully proud of), with a Canadian cousin, "Annie Laurie," who sang Scotch ballads so bonnily. Then came "Puck and Paul," as they called us; lastly (he always is last), "the boy Johnnie," with Puck's sweet little sister, Ariel.

That morning I put in the hardest work I ever did in my life. A wind got up with the sun and blew on land—blew and blew, and wiped us on shore every half hour. We had not yet got our muscles and joints "greased up" for business, and it went very hard with us. Puck worked like a galley slave; she knelt up in the bow and plowed against the wind with all the determination that has pulled John Bull through so many glorious battles. At 11 o'clock we had discarded our collars, caps and shoes and had got down to hard pan, for neither of us would give in. Puck did most of the paddling, I devoting all my attention and muscle to keeping the bow into the wind. I was not brilliantly successful, for despite my efforts we drifted; but everyone else drifted also, and Norton touched shore oftener than we did. Every half hour the boy Johnnie suggested a layoff. "On account of the girls, you know," he said. "It's too deuced hard on Puck and Paul." But we saw through him. Johnnie is the laziest drone about going upstream or against wind or portaging that I ever saw.

In the face of it all we never halted until 12 o'clock, and then, I admit, everyone was "played out." The joke of it was Norton gave in first, so Puck and I gave him the laugh and Hampstead roasted him a good deal. I like Hampstead. He learned to paddle in fewer lessons than anyone I ever taught, and yet he took it so much as a matter of course and never talked or "blew" about it, except on that single occasion, and then I encouraged him because it was so droll to see a greenhorn paddler "down" a man who thought himself the feather of our canoe club.

Well, we pitched canvas in a lovely spot and decided to remain there until the next day, and after making an enormous hole in the hamper Puck and I each took a blanket and went off by ourselves to "commune with nature," as we told the others. We communed rather practically, inasmuch as we slept through sheer exhaustion from 2:30 until 6:15 P.M., when Mrs. Norton came and awoke us and told us tea was ready, nice hot tea and fried bacon and strawberry jam and buttered bread; also that she wondered we were not afraid of snakes and bears and all sorts of things, the idea of us lying asleep there alone without telling some of them to keep watch! We did not care for snakes, we were too tired to care for elephants if they happened to come that way, but we did care for tea, and after it we made love to Johnnie and Hampstead, and got them to "wash up."

Before we went on that cruise I had always slept on a stretcher while under canvas, but when we first spoke of the trip and Puck was inquiring, among other things, about sleeping accommodation, I said: "Oh, don't worry about that! My forefathers surely knew the secret of the happiest and healthiest way of tenting. You can't take stretchers in a canoe, you know; so just roll yourself up in a blanket, tuck a cushion under your head and—snooze." After that I was ashamed to go back on my ancestors' method the first night in camp and in the very territory they invaded and fought through and won their greatest victories in years and years ago. I pretended not to hear poor little Puck groan now and again through the night when she rolled against a particularly rugged point in the rock whereon we had pitched. I even pretended not to hear myself groan.

But after that night the rocks seemed to grow tired of

investigating Puck's pretty pink, English flesh, and my Native anatomy seemed to relax and accommodate its surface to the roughest conglomeration of sticks and stones. I suppose, really, we got used to it.

We struck camp at sunrise the following day and paddled across the remaining six miles of the lake, which was calm as a millpond. Then through a little lagoon, beyond which opened out a larger lake than the one we had just covered. It was a very beautiful sheet of water, sprinkled with islands, wild, lone, and as uninhabited as the North Pole. The near shore loomed up a solid wall of gray stone, but from waterline to summit, as clean and bare as if a giant knife had sliced through its massive centre, leaving one-half upright, burying the other beneath the black, still waters that rippled only to the cutting of our bows, to the dipping of our blades. We paddled up close to the pitiless shore—what a hopeless place it was wherein to meet a storm.

How fragile and insecure seemed that wee canoe of ours! How helpless and insignificant were we two girls paddling alone under the frown of that monster rock, over the bosom of that deceptively placid lake! We slipped noiselessly along, awed and silenced, but fearful never. What was there to fear with the sunshine glinting, the sky laughing blue above, the winds a-slumbering, and, moreover, with Norton's red and black blazer far to forward, and with Hampstead's heavenly baritone floating away among the distant islands as he sang:

And oh! the bird, my darling,
Was singing of you—of you.

and with Johnnie shouting, "Hold on!" every ten minutes from half a mile astern of us?

It took us two days to cover that lake, at the end of which time Puck and I had an experience.

Having camped on the islands, and drunk irony lake water for forty-eight hours, we hailed a spring with delight. It was near the portage which we had to make into the river, and although we lunched beside it there was no suitable spot near on which we could stretch canvas, so we went on downstream about 3 miles to camp for our last night in the lake region. Before leaving it, however, Norton put some black bottles that had white labels on them, a pot of marmalade and a bowl of butter into the spring to get "conditioned," and said we could easily paddle back for them before supper.

Norton is the greatest man you ever saw to make future arrangements and leave someone else to carry them out. At 5 o'clock Norton said: "Say, you boys, don't you think it's time to go back after the stuff in the spring? I'll build the fire for supper, and fix down these guy ropes. They don't seem steady, so that'll let you out of all the work, and you'll just have the fun of the paddle."

Johnnie said his back was "awful sore; he had strained it somehow." Hampstead had taken himself off for a swim, so, as it had clouded up a little and was cool, Puck and I said we would go if the girls would get tea and "wash up." Agreed. So we started off, got the stuff, and then I made Puck turn around and lounge facing me, as it was mere child's play for me to sit there and steer home with the current. We had run about a mile when Puck told me to look around at the odd, pretty cloud that was coming up. I looked, and nearly fell out of the canoe with fright; it was one of those straight ridges of squall cloud that come around the corner at 2:40 pace and that seem to haunt these northern latitudes.

"Is it not pretty?" said Puck; "the edge is so clearly defined and ragged, and oh! look, it seems to be all boiling over."

"Very pretty," I assented, as I steered inshore.

"Oh, are you going to land? Don't you think we ought to get back as soon as possible? It might rain on us," said my dear, innocent little foreigner comrade.

"It might," I again assented in tones of desperate calm. "If you have a dry stitch on you, Puck, in three minutes you may thank the celerity with which you can crawl under a canoe." You never have to explain things to Puck, she understands by intuition, and is never surprised by what she sees. It took us but a moment to beach, scramble out, empty and haul up the canoe and turn it upside down, bottom to windward. Then came a dull roar of wind through the forest behind us, followed by a whirl of leaves and a dash of freshening air, and down splashed the drops—great, generous drops that never struck the same spot twice, because they didn't have to. Exit Puck under the canoe, pulling her heels in after her, followed by Paul, the cushions, "white labels," marmalade and butter, and there we lay tangled up in the thwarts for an hour, while Puck recited Browning and I fanned the audience with my "cow's breakfast," and the heavens turned on their water taps and apparently pointed the hose straight at the bottom of our boat. The hottest place I know of is under a canoe in a summer shower, and it is the crookedest place, too; your back gets a kink in it and your neck gets warped with the heat, and the first thing you do when the rain is over is to get out on all fours and stretch and smooth out your ankles and elbows.

We never knew until afterward how Hampstead had organized himself into a search party and paddled up the river in his bathing suit to rescue us, or how wild the poor boy was when he found neither bottles nor girls and could not see through the pelting rain our little gray boat tucked away among the trees. He wandered about the river all through the storm, and we ran across him just at dark when we were nearing the camp. I never saw a man so delighted (and so wet) in my life; he had given us up as dead. Ariel was wringing her hands when we landed, and "Annie Laurie" was wringing the rainwater out of the whole camping outfit. Mrs. Norton was parading the shore, crazy with anxiety, while Norton and Johnnie were reconstructing the tents which had blown down, and Norton was saying: "Oh, shut up, girls; you can just bet Puck and Paul and the *Wildcat* are safe enough. I only hope those white labels are." Norton is inhumanly hard-hearted.

The next day we sailed for 7 miles before a light, brisk breeze. Then the course of the river turned, and it almost blew a head wind; we would have had to do so much tacking that we hauled down the canvas and took to paddles once more. I am not an expert sailor, and Puck knows nothing at all about it. Of course Mrs. Norton did not wish us to hoist a scrap of canvas, and wanted to tow us, but dear old Norton backed me up as usual, and as I promised to keep very close to the boys, I got my own way. The wind was too strong for me to sail my usual fashion, with the sheet in my teeth, while I steered with a paddle, so we loaded our kit in the bow, and Puck lay amidships, with her feet braced against the bow thwart, and held the sheet, while half of her weight hung over the windward gunwale.

We ran our first rapids, too, that day. They were glorious. Oh! those indescribably splendid rapids that throng the far inland rivers of Canada, that swirl, scurry and scamper among their stones, whose voices whisper along velvet shores, then break into rollicking laughter as they dash on their immovable boulders and split into a million bubbles that fall and float away like countless unset pearls.

It was just such a rapid that lay before us that afternoon, not a very perilous one, but one that required vigilance, nerve and pluck to face; a rapid whose dash of danger flew to one's head like wine and fascinated you into a daring recklessness. Norton led, Hampstead next—it was the first really good rapid he had ever steered through. Then came we girls bounding along, with Johnnie 50 yards astern, to pick us out in case we spilt. We swerved around boulders like a boomerang, shipping occasionally and being deluged with spray. Puck sat steady as a rock. What a picture she was dressed in her navy blue serge, with its white flannel Byron collar, a white "tam" tilted over her pretty, curly head, her lovely, clever little face reflecting all the moods of that wild, harum-scarum river!

It was to be our last night under canvas; so we camped just below the rapids, where afar downstream we could see the lumberyards and sawmills of the backwoods station where we were to start for home by rail the following day.

"Well, girls," said Norton, as we sat around the campfire after tea, "you haven't done badly; 80 miles in a canoe—without a man—and nary a mishap is not an everyday occurrence—here's to you, lassies, here's to the Paddle Princesses," and he pulled the cork of the last white label; then the boys and girls sang "For they are jolly good fellows," where we smiled blushingly through our sunburn and patted each other on the shoulder. And we all quieted down then with a certain homesickness that it would soon be over; we watched the sun set off behind ragged birch trees that twinkled their nervous leaves all over the west aflame to blood color; the campfire weakened and paled beneath that bit of glorious sky which blazed in a beauty that overflowed the clouds and dashed its fullness in the river's depths, where the rapids deluged the gray old boulders with wine-colored spray and purpled in the shadows of nightfall. Nightfall crept closer and closer from out the black cedars and laid its tender fingers on our tired eyes, bringing dreams of snarling rapids that swung our canoe like a cradle; of cool, fresh spray dashing over our sunburnt faces; and of soft and distant music made by waters whispering, swirling, murmuring beneath the northern stars.

Annie Peck, her two Swiss guides, and a professor en route to Peck's first attempt on Mount Illampu in Bolivia, from her book A Search for the Apex of America.

3

CONQUERING MOUNT HUASCARAN

Annie Smith Peck

(1850–1935)

> *The chief joy is the varied and perfect*
> *exercise, in the midst of noble scenery*
> *and exhilarating atmosphere, for the*
> *attainment of an object, the conquest of*
> *the mountain. The peak utters*
> *a challenge. The climber responds by*
> *saying to himself, "I can and I will*
> *conquer it."*

The notion of conquest appears often in mountaineering literature, particularly in narratives written by early climbers in the nineteenth century, most of whom were men. But Annie Smith Peck's aspirations were no different from those of her male counterparts. Her words here reveal that her search for adventure was defined as overcoming adversity, achieving a record, and attaining recognition. She also set out to prove that a woman can do what a man can do.

Annie Peck came to mountaineering relatively late in life, although she developed her competitive spirit as a youngster who was challenged to keep up with three older brothers. She was born into a prosperous and conservative family in Providence, Rhode Island, on October 19, 1850. She attended a school for young ladies, graduated from a teacher preparation school, and, as she had not yet married, began to teach.

But at age twenty-four she turned abruptly from the norm. Her brothers had attended university, and she wanted to attend, too. The moment of decision came one day as she was putting on her shoes. She put on one shoe. "But I'll be twenty-seven when I graduate!" she told herself. She put on the other shoe. "Well, you'll be twenty-seven anyhow!" Age would not deter her from her goal—a harbinger of decisions to come. She enrolled at the University of Michigan, which had begun to accept female students only four years before, majoring in Greek classics and graduating with honors in all subjects. She earned a master of art degree by examination, taught Latin and elocution at the college level for two years, then studied in Germany and Athens, where she was the first woman to attend the American School of Classical Studies.

While in Europe, she traveled by the Matterhorn and was awestruck. "On beholding this majestic awe-inspiring peak, I felt that I should never be happy until I, too, should scale those frowning walls which have beckoned so many upwards, a few to their destruction." She could not afford the necessary equipment or fees for guides, but the mountain called to her. To satisfy her urge to climb, Peck scaled several lesser mountains in Switzerland and Greece, but she would have to return for the Matterhorn. Her immediate and deeply felt draw to a mountain is not atypical in the world of mountaineering.

A core of women climbers were making a name for themselves in Europe in the second half of the nineteenth century. Between 1859 and 1879, for example, England's Lucy Walker climbed almost 100 peaks, including the feared and respected Matterhorn (14,782 feet) in 1871. Meta Brevoort, an American, followed on the Matterhorn a few days later. Mary Mummery, Mrs. E. P. Jackson, Lily Bristow, and Elizabeth Le Blond, among others, also made notable ascents in the Alps. Mountaineering was a well-established activity in Europe, and although women had to break into the male club at least there was a club to break into. In the United States, however, mountaineering was still in its infancy. When Julia Archibald Homes climbed Pikes Peak in 1858, Isabella Bird climbed Longs Peak in 1873, and Fay Fuller climbed Mount Rainier in 1890, theirs were isolated efforts.

After her European tour Peck headed back to the United States to teach Latin at Smith College. To earn extra money she lectured privately on Roman and Greek archaeology. In between teaching and lecturing, she tackled successively more challenging mountains, climbing Cloud's Rest (almost 10,000 feet) in Yosemite and Mount Shasta (14,442 feet) in northern California in 1888 when she was thirty-eight. Of Shasta she said, "The exercise was delightful and invigorating."

By 1892 Peck's parlor lectures in private homes were doing so well that she decided to leave teaching and live off her lecture fees. In a letter negotiating payment for a lecture, Peck showed her practical side, one that resurfaced as she struggled to raise money and gather equipment for her expeditions: "When I cannot get what I want I sometimes take what I can get."

Peck still had the Matterhorn on her list, and she returned to Europe in 1895, where she climbed several other peaks and arranged for two guides (standard for the day) to take her up the Matterhorn. While she waited for good weather she received a letter from her family that stiffened her resolve: "If you are determined to commit suicide, why not come home and do so in a quiet, lady-like manner." Her family had been generally unsupportive of all of her "unladylike" activities, from attending university to climbing. Only her oldest brother encouraged her.

The climb went smoothly. Ironically, Peck was less noted as the third woman to climb the mountain than as the first woman to climb it in pants (her predecessors, Lucy Walker and Meta Brevoort, climbed in dresses). Peck later wrote:

> Men, we all know, climb in knickerbockers. Ordinary trousers are too cumbersome. Women, on the contrary, will declare that a skirt is no hindrance to their locomotion. This is obviously absurd, and though a few ladies have climbed mountains like the Matterhorn in extremely scant and abbreviated skirts, I dare assert that suitably made knickerbockers (not so scant as men's and yet not too full) are not only more comfortable but more becoming, whether to stout or slender figures . . . for a woman in difficult mountaineering to waste her strength and endanger her life with a skirt is foolish in the extreme.

Peck also addressed the issue of a certain undergarment: "It may not be necessary to add that no one should climb mountains or even hills in corsets."

Upon her return to the United States, Peck began billing herself on lecture placards as the "Queen of the Climbers" and looking for ways to support her mountaineering interests. One strategy to gain financial backing was to make news by achieving an altitude record or becoming the first woman to climb a peak. She persuaded the *New York World* to pay for a trip to Mexico in 1897. There she climbed Orizaba (18,885 feet)—briefly earning the world altitude record for women—and then Popocatépetl, which had never been climbed by a woman.

By 1900 Peck had hired someone to manage her lecture tours. Talks on archaeology had given way to lectures on mountaineering. "Mountain climbing, I thought, might be a more popular theme, and by telling the story of my adventure I could conscientiously pursue this diversion." She was careful to bill herself as "Miss Annie Peck" so people would realize a single woman held the spotlight.

At the turn of the twentieth century Peck became a charter member in the American Alpine Club and attended the Congrès International de l'Alpinisme in Paris as a U.S. delegate. While in Europe she climbed peaks in Austria, Italy, and Switzerland.

Peck's attention turned more and more to serious record setting. "My next thought was to do a little genuine exploration, to conquer a virgin peak, to attain some height where no *man* had previously stood." (The italics are Peck's.) She was "from earliest years a firm believer in the equality of the sexes" and felt that "any great achievement in any line of endeavor would be of advantage to my sex."

This goal led Peck to South America, where there were scores of unclimbed peaks. She first tackled a mountain in Bolivia—Illampu, also called Sorata—but the expedition was fraught with difficulties. One of her two Swiss guides was afraid of the local porters. The professor who was to give the expedition credibility left earlier than planned. The porters viewed the professor as the expedition leader and would not do as Peck requested. In despair, she abandoned the attempt. "Never before had I felt so helpless. To manage three men seemed beyond my power. Perhaps some of my more experienced married sisters would have done better." Peck was not strong enough to carry her own equipment—not even her climbing irons (crampons)—so she needed men to help her accomplish her goals, but she had been unable to convince them that she was the leader.

Peck decamped to New York and began raising funds for another expedition. She sought advances from newspapers for future articles and set up the Andean Exploration Society, asking $5 per member. In a pamphlet advertising the society she explained: "Especially should those who desire the recognition of woman's ability in whatever direction be disposed to encourage one who in an unusual line has already achieved large success and shown capabilities far beyond those of most men." In other words, Peck was saying, "If you support the idea that women can achieve, support me because I've achieved more than most men climbers." She secured $1,200, enough to go back to South America but not enough to afford Swiss guides. On this and following expeditions Peck made do with what she had when she could not get what she wanted.

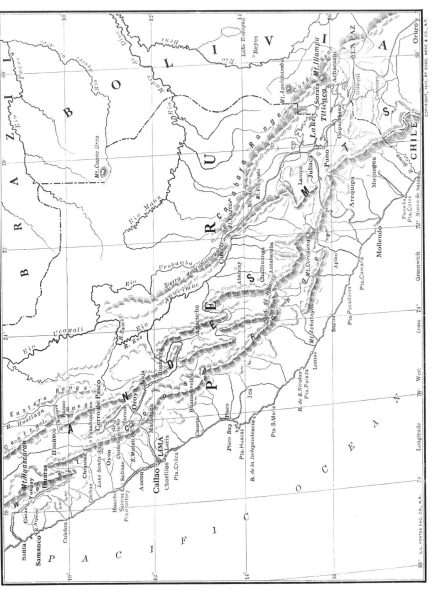

Annie Peck's expeditions to South America, from A Search for the Apex of America.

Peck sporting the outfit she wore the day she reached the summit of Mount Huascaran, from A Search for the Apex of America.

Peck returned to La Paz, Bolivia, in 1904. Her earlier experience on Mount Illampu made her doubt that she could deal with her porters, and she may have felt she needed a male escort to maintain propriety. She hired an Austrian in La Paz to accompany her to Illampu. Unfortunately, Peck could not manage the Austrian any better than she had her previous colleagues. At one point she climbed upward, only to find that he had untied himself from the rope, leaving her dangerously unprotected. Had she slipped, she could have been injured—or killed. She gave up on Illampu, bitterly disappointed.

Looking for another challenge, Peck focused on Mount Huascaran in Peru, deciding it was probably higher than Mount Illampu anyway. (Many South American peaks had not been mapped or measured.) She went to Peru to check out the double-peaked Huascaran and decided to give it a try, but she encountered one frustration after another. On the first attempt she signed up a man she met in a hotel lobby to accompany her; with no climbing experience he was more of a liability than an asset. Desperate, she then went up without a male associate, but the porters had inadequate clothing and refused to go on. Peck returned to New York.

By 1906 Peck had scraped together enough funds to embark again for Peru. Once there, she located a charming man who the locals said was *loco*. He was of no use to her in two attempts on Huascaran. With mutinous porters and an unstable companion, she felt lucky to get back alive.

It was clearer than ever before that Peck needed real guides to accompany her, and she was as determined as ever to climb Huascaran. Her next round of fund-raising was more successful, and she collected enough money to hire Rudolf Taugwalder and Gabriel Zumtaugwald, reputable guides from Switzerland.

On Peck's fifth attempt to climb Huascaran, Taugwalder suffered from altitude sickness and had to turn back. Zumtaugwald performed valiantly but could not do the work of two men, and he and Peck were forced to retreat just two hours shy of the summit. After resting at the nearest village, the three tried once more. The day of their final attempt dawned bone-chillingly cold, and Peck needed every stitch of clothing she owned, including a knit face mask with a painted mustache she had purchased locally.

Peck chronicled the harrowing events on the mountain that day in an article published in 1909 (see "The Most Dramatic Event in My Life," following), as well as in her book, *A Search for the Apex of America: High Mountain Climbing in Peru and Bolivia Including the Conquest of Huascaran*. Peck was fifty-eight when she reached the summit of Huascaran, but for reasons of her own she never mentioned her age.

After her return to the United States, Peck was asked whether she would climb again. Her recent difficulties were still fresh in her mind, and she answered: "Surely I hope again to climb, for pleasure merely, smaller mountains such as the Alps and Canadian Rockies; while if funds were provided, I would gladly make further exploration among the many untrodden peaks of the Andes, the Himalayas, or elsewhere, with full equipment and competent assistants, prepared to make more accurate scientific observations than were possible on my last expedition. But never, no, never, shall I again set out so meagerly financed and equipped as to be compelled to serve as porter, cook, photographer, scientific man, and general boss, all at the same time!"

Her return should have been triumphant, but it was marred by controversy. One report about the climb said that Peck's carelessness, not Taugwalder's, had been responsible for his frostbite. Also, Peck had been unable to measure the height of the mountain, so she estimated it. "If, as seems probable, the height is 24,000 feet, I have the honor of breaking the world's record for men as well as women." With these words she ignited a firestorm.

In 1906 Fanny Bullock Workman, a wealthy alpinist and explorer from Massachusetts who was climbing in the Himalayas with her husband, had climbed a peak that was almost 23,000 feet high. Workman was horrified to learn that another woman was claiming her altitude record for women. She spent $13,000 to send three French engineers to Peru to triangulate Huascaran's height, dispensing more than four times what Peck had spent on her entire expedition.

The engineers calculated the north peak—the one Peck had climbed—to be 21,812 feet. Workman firmly held the world record for women. Peck had set a record, but it was the less prestigious (although still worthy) altitude record for an American in the Western Hemisphere. When the American Alpine Club registered official support of Workman's claim Peck felt betrayed, and although she had been with the club since its inception she resigned.

The year *A Search for the Apex of America* was published (1911), Peck made one more first ascent in South America, climbing Mount

Coropuna in Peru. She planted a flag proclaiming "Votes for Women" on the summit.

After Coropuna her focus began to shift from mountaineering to travel. She chronicled her adventures in *The South American Tour* (1913) and published *Industrial and Commercial South America* (1922) to encourage good economic relations between the United States and South America. She toured South America by air in 1929 and 1930, a time when it was grueling just to be a passenger. Amelia Earhart endorsed Peck's book *Flying over South America,* saying, "I am only following in the footsteps of one who pioneered when it was brave just to put on the bloomers necessary for mountain-climbing."

For long stretches Peck's address was that of her publisher. When she was in New York she stayed in a hotel, not an apartment or a home. When someone asked her where her home was, she answered simply, "Where my trunk is."

Peck became a Fellow of the Royal Geographical Society in 1917 and a member of the Society of Woman Geographers in 1928. In 1928 the Lima Geographical Society named the north peak of Huascaran "Cumbre Ana Peck" in her honor. The "Ana" was included to show that the peak had been climbed by a woman.

At age eighty-two, Peck climbed New Hampshire's Mount Madison (5,363 feet), but her doctors feared for her health and she climbed no more. Restless for adventure, she continued to travel. Three years later, in 1935, she set out on a two-month world tour but was forced to turn back. She died of pneumonia shortly thereafter. She had spent her life breaking ground not only for herself but also for others of her gender. Annie Smith Peck was a self-made woman whose inner strength carried her through life and its many challenges. The fact that she suffered from being a front-runner was inevitable; that she persevered is admirable.

The Most Dramatic Event in My Life

Whenever, hitherto, I have been asked to relate my most thrilling experience in mountain climbing I have always been tempted to respond that I never had any. True, I had dangled over a precipice where the landing place was 5,000 feet below; but that was of no consequence, as I had a good grip on a stout rope which was fastened with an iron clamp to the rock above, and, further, there was another rope around my waist by which the stalwart guide a moment later pulled me back where I belonged.

This adventure did not arouse a qualm, for there was no real danger. A person who would be disturbed by such an episode—one who is subject to thrills—is out of place on a difficult mountain and is rarely found there. Climbing, properly done, is for the most part safely done. It is somewhat perilous to live at all, but among the Andes for the greater part of the time I have considered myself safer than on the streets of our great metropolis.

Not all of the time, however, and the story of those exciting hours I will now relate. The experience which nearly cost us our lives was the result of an unexpected combination of circumstances when scaling that great fortress of nature, Mount Huascaran, in South America.

It was the day of my final triumph, when, after ten years' planning and effort, on my fourth visit to South America, I at last attained the goal of my ambition, the summit of a gigantic peak, hitherto untrod, the loftiest mountain on this hemisphere—perhaps the highest point where man had stood in the whole world. I ought to have been happy, but I was not—not half so happy as when, two years earlier, I stood alone on the top of a fine peak near the source of the Amazon River, 200 miles to the south. Though

ANNIE SMITH PECK

this was a mere trifle in comparison with what I had planned to do, it was a first ascent, the conquest of a virgin peak 600 or 800 feet higher than Mont Blanc, the monarch of the Alps, and I had climbed it alone, my companions remaining below until they found that I had actually reached the summit. The prospect was delightful; the return would be as easy as the ascent.

But on Huascaran it was different. My chief thought was, "I am here at last, but shall we ever get down again!" With me were two stalwart Swiss guides, who, it might be supposed, would afford ample assistance, yet when making a previous attempt on the mountain, Rudolf, the elder of the two guides, had suffered so severely from mountain sickness that he had turned back at an altitude of 16,000 feet, leaving the rest of us to struggle on for days, to turn back at last two hours below the summit, lest we never live to tell the story of our victory. Eighteen days after, I again climbed that final peak rising 4,000 feet above the saddle, where on both occasions we had made our highest camp; since, on the icy slopes above, slanting at 40, 50 or 60 degrees, seamed with caverns, crevasses and perpendicular walls, there was no room to pitch a tent 9 feet square. We must climb it and return in a single day.

We should have started earlier on this long and dangerous journey, but all had worked hard the two days preceding. The night and early morning were very cold, with a high wind blowing. I had therefore thought it wiser to postpone the ascent another day 'til the wind should abate to some extent and we were in better condition to undertake the journey. Rudolf and Gabriel, however, were anxious to set out, declaring that it might be less windy higher up. This was improbable, yet, against my better judgment, I yielded to their wishes.

The first unfortunate circumstance was the condition of the mountain. The snow had been hard enough on our first attempt to necessitate the cutting of steps, but it was not very smooth. Now, the unusual cold had made it still harder and the high wind had blown from the exposed slopes all the lighter particles, leaving a surface smooth as glass, such as Gabriel said he had never seen in Switzerland, except in small patches. Another misfortune was the loss of an Eskimo suit, loaned to me by the American Museum of Natural History; this, alas! had been lost on our previous descent of a great ice wall 300 feet high, where, as our packs were being lowered by a rope, one had slipped away and disappeared into an unfathomable abyss. So I could but put on all the clothing I had and hope for the best; three suits of woolen underwear, tights, knickerbockers, a woolen face mask against the wind, two flannel waists and two sweaters, but all of these were more or less porous and not adequate in keeping out the wind.

The second link in the chain of accidents was as follows: On setting out in the morning my mittens of vicuna (the warmest and softest of furs) became too warm, so I replaced them with one pair of woolen mittens and another of mitts. The fur mittens, too large for my pockets, I gave to Rudolf to place in his rucksack. Later, where we were more exposed to the wind, my hands grew cold, so I requested Rudolf to give me the fur mittens. Taking those with some black armlets from his rucksack, he tucked the former under one arm, and said, "Which will you have first?" I wanted to exclaim, "Look out you don't lose my mittens!" But, like most men, the guides were rather impatient at what they considered unnecessary advice from a woman, even an employer, so I refrained and said, "Give me the armlets." The next moment he exclaimed, "I have lost one of your mittens!" I did not see it go, but anything dropped on that steep, smooth slope, even without the high wind, might as well have gone over a precipice. I was indeed angry and alarmed, but it was no time to talk. I could do that after we got down.

The best I could do now was to put the one fur mitten on my right hand, which, carrying the ice-ax, was the more exposed, and the two woolen mittens and one mit on my left hand. These served for a time, but when at last we reached the long, almost horizontal ridge at the top of the north peak and were proceeding to the farther and highest point, I suddenly realized that my left hand was insensible and freezing. Snatching off my mittens I found the hand nearly black. I caught up some snow and rubbed it vigorously. In a few moments it began to ache, which signified that circulation was restored. I replaced the mittens, but it would evidently freeze again, for it was now three o'clock and would soon be still colder. Luckily, I had been overcautious in having Gabriel bring up a poncho, a heavy woolen shawl or blanket with a slit in the middle to slip the head through, fearing I might be cold when we halted for luncheon or on the summit. To this I owe the present possession of my left hand, for by protecting my hand somewhat and keeping my whole body warmer, it rendered good service. But it was awkward to wear, reaching nearly to my knees, and was the cause of my slipping and almost of my death on the way down.

Owing to the fact that I did not dare expose my hand too much to the wind, I was unable to shield the hypsometer from the blast sufficiently for Gabriel to light the candle with which to boil the water for the determination of the altitude. After striking twenty matches we decided to give it up. It was a terrible disappointment, to have broken, perhaps, the world's record and not to be able to prove it, but my life was to me of still greater importance. We went on to the summit, where I took snapshots with my camera in all four directions, and then turned downward. It was not a moment for rejoicing. The time for that would be when we were down again. Higher, perchance, than anyone had ever been, except possibly in a balloon with death resulting to most of the party, 4 miles and a half above the level of the sea, nearly four times as high as the summit of Mt. Washington, we did not enjoy the view, being too high and also too cold.

Half past three! Soon it would be dark. Seven hours coming up! Would it take as many to get down? Steep rocks or icy slopes are more dangerous to descend than to go up, and after nightfall far more perilous. So, without a moment's rest, we began to retrace our steps. The summit ridge, a quarter of a mile or more in length, was quickly traversed, but at the end of the ridge our difficulties began.

Gabriel had led nearly all the way up, cutting most of the steps. Rudolf had gone up second so that he could hold the rope for me while Gabriel cut the steps. On the way down it was deemed safer for me to go in the middle, Rudolf taking the lead, and Gabriel the more responsible position in the rear; for, in descending, this is the post of honor, the strongest and most skillful of the party being expected to stand firm and hold the rope in case one in front shall slip. If he goes, as a rule, all are lost. A Swiss guide, however, is not expected to slip, and very rarely does. Their shoes were well studded with nails, while mine were not, as I had expected to wear climbing irons which would make them unnecessary. This time, however, I had not worn climbing irons because they are fastened with straps which impede the circulation, and on the previous ascent I had one foot frostbitten and did not wish to risk freezing my foot solid and having it cut off, as it would be more susceptible the second time up, but now

ANNIE SMITH PECK

I regretted that the irons had not been brought, for the steps were very small indeed. The big steps which my guide had made on the Jungfrau required from ten to twenty blows each, but this would not do on the long slope of Huascaran. Two or three hacks were all that Gabriel could give, so the steps were not half as large as his toes. It was enough coming up, but going down it was terrifying.

A smooth slope of 60 degrees is never pleasant. I feared the outcome greatly, but we had to go down and the faster the better. We had not gone far when I saw something black fly away. It was one of Rudolf's mittens. Later he said that he laid it down to fasten his shoe and it blew away. After dark, he lost his other mitten, changing it from one hand to the other, which was so numb then that he did not feel the mitten dropping off. I, however, was the first to slip. Gabriel above held the rope tight so that I slid but a few feet and was able at once to regain my footing.

Some time after dark it seemed advisable for Gabriel to take the lead. There was a long traverse amid crevasses, caverns and appalling slopes across the wide flank of the mountain. Now the moon was just behind me, casting a shadow over the place where I must step. The poncho would often sway in the wind, as I was in the act of stepping, so as to conceal the spot where I must place my foot. I had previously thought myself sure-footed, and my eye for distance is good; but now my foot missed the exact spot so that I fell, as usual, in the sitting posture, crying out to warn the guides. I expected nothing serious. What, then, was my horror to find that thus sitting I was sliding down that glassy slope! We were all nearly in the same line, so I slid 15 or 20 feet before the rope held. Now to get back! The guides called to me to get up, but I was all in a heap, the rope tight around my waist, and unable to move. So the men came together just above and hauled me up the slope. Thankful once more to be in the line of steps I started onward, resolved to be more careful. But again I slipped and again slid far below. Each time my terror increased. It seemed that the way would never end! I begged Gabriel to stop for the night in some cavern or crevasse, saying that we should never get down alive, but he refused to listen and kept on. Had we halted, we should have frozen.

Once when I slipped I was astonished to see Rudolf dart by me far below. I did not dream that he had slipped, but wondered how he could assist me by running down there. Later, I learned that he did slip, and only the strength and resolution of Gabriel saved us all from destruction. I was astonished later to hear that Rudolf never expected to get down alive. But hands and one foot being frozen, he naturally had not firm footing. Gabriel said that he never despaired except when Rudolf slipped. Then he thought we were all lost. But he stood firm, though two fingers were caught between the rope and his ice-ax, for he knew it was life or death. Had *he* given way, after sliding some distance we should all have dropped off thousands of feet below.

At last, *at last,* Gabriel paused and said, "Now we are safe. If you like, you can slide." Happy was I to know that we had passed out from among those dreadful abysses and appalling slopes to the moderate one just above our camp and that we were out of danger. I sat down and slid rapidly toward the tent, bumping and floundering, Gabriel holding the rope, 'til I upset and was almost annihilated. It was half past ten when at length we found refuge in the tent, too tired to eat or sleep, with nothing to drink, but thankful at last for rest and safety.

A young Dora Keen, from World's Work, *1913.*

4

A THIRST FOR ADVENTURE
Dora Keen
(1871–1963)

*A new feeling of confidence, a new zest
came over me each day as I realized what
a woman might do in America. Sure of
respect and of every assistance, in Alaska
at least, her limitations need be only
those within herself, her measure that of
which she is capable, her development in
her own hands to make or mar.*

 **Dora Keen glanced at a** U.S. Geological Survey report as she sat in a prospector's cabin on the Kenai Peninsula in Alaska. Mount Blackburn in the Wrangell Range had never been ascended, it said, and the mountain was "worthy of the hardiest mountaineer." The brief description changed Keen's life, for she decided then and there to climb the peak.

The dotted line indicates Dora Keen and her two guides' route up the Wellenkuffe, a mountain in the Alps, from National Geographic, *1911.*

It was 1911, and the forty-year-old Keen had set out for Alaska to get a look at the "last pioneer region of America." She traveled first to the Kenai Peninsula, where she went on several camping trips, climbed mountains, and searched for Kodiak bear. She intended to head back to the southwest coast to see the glaciers and mountains by boats and trains "merely as a tourist." But Keen was traveling alone and could do as she pleased, and she wanted to climb Mount Blackburn.

Keen was an experienced mountaineer. She had climbed in the Selkirks in Canada, the Dolomites in Italy, Chimborazo in Ecuador, Mount Whitney in California, volcanoes in Mexico, and various mountains in Norway. She had spent a month in the Austrian Alps in 1909—ascending ten peaks, including the Matterhorn—and another month in the French Alps the following summer. As in Annie Peck's time, the Alps were considered the true training ground for mountaineering, with the Matterhorn the test piece.

Keen's motives for climbing were simple. She pursued climbing "for the wonderful views and the vigorous exertion, for the relaxation of

Dora Keen scales the Dent du Requin in the French Alps in 1910, from National Geographic, *1911.*

a complete change for mind and body, and because of the inspiration to the spirit. . . . To me, mountain climbing is a sport that is worthwhile in it-self—to those who enjoy it—apart from any question of fame or of new achievement. My objects have been nei-ther." Keen did note, however, that combining "exploration with mountaineering must, no doubt, so increase the in-terest as to well repay the aug-mented difficulties."

The difficulties on Black-burn were indeed augmented. Previously, Keen had hired guides to lead her up the routes and ensure her safety. Now she would be the expedi-tion leader and would assume responsibility for the safety of others. Moreover, climbing in Alaska was more like exploring in the Arc-tic than climbing in civilized areas. The area around Mount Blackburn was uninhabited, with no hotels at the base of the climb and no huts along the way, as there had been in Europe. Treeline in Alaska was rela-tively low, which meant Keen would have to carry significantly more fuel than usual. Snowline was also low, necessitating more travel over snow. There were more hours of sunlight than in lower latitudes, leaving less time to travel over hardened snow and thus avoid avalanches.

Tackling an unclimbed, virtually unknown mountain in the wilderness of Alaska without trained guides was a daring undertaking for anyone, male or female. When the Italian Duke of the Abruzzi had climbed Mount Saint Elias in the Yukon fourteen years earlier, his party included several well-known climbers, a doctor, four Italian mountain guides, and a large crew of porters. Keen intended to hire a handful of locals.

She recruited R. F. McClellan, former superintendent of the Bonanza Mine in Kennicott, to lead her party, and he rounded up three tough, reliable prospectors—none of whom had climbed before but all of whom were used to cold weather and rugged duty. Another man would handle the horses, which transported gear the first 15 miles. Dogs were used to pull poles for tents and cots. Keen added to the party a German from Cordova who knew how to handle a rope and cut steps in the ice. He assured her that even if everyone else were to turn back, he would continue to the summit with her.

Keen had her own ice ax and crampons, but her men needed gear, too. None was available in Alaska: "No one ropes in Alaska, nor are ice axes known. When a man perishes in a crevasse, the glacier is named for him," Keen noted. The boat to Seattle ran only once a week, and the trip took four days each way. Keen was eager to begin her expedition, so blacksmiths at the mine and in Cordova made ice axes and "creepers" (instep crampons) for the men.

The expedition set forth on August 15. It took the group four days to wrestle a huge sled loaded with 750 pounds of food and gear along the Kennicott Glacier to the base of Mount Blackburn. The going was so difficult that the German climber turned back.

On one of those early evenings, Keen and two others hunted mountain goats for food for the dogs. The hunt was unsuccessful, but the experience was important for Keen because she earned the respect of the men. "If you can follow them goats, I guess you can climb Mount Blackburn," one of them said. That was high praise from the prospectors, and their acceptance bolstered Keen's confidence. "I had come to Alaska on a voyage of discovery," she wrote later. "Being alone had seemed to put every limitation in my way, and now, on the contrary, my love of adventure and sport could be satisfied as never before, because of the character of the men of Alaska. I was actually launched on an expedition of my own, the most adventurous and hazardous I could desire, yet sure of being cared for in safety with consideration and respect."

For three days Keen took on the role of command central in base camp while the men split into groups to probe Mount Blackburn for a route to the summit. The only safe time to travel was between 3 A.M., when it got light, and 9 A.M, when avalanches forced them off the slope. At last two men found a route they thought would work, and the party set off on the ninth day.

The season was against them. The sun triggered relentless avalanches and made the snow mushy; it was a struggle to move 10 feet. Ice walls hemmed them in. Gaping crevasses threatened at every step. When they could get off the ice onto rock they experienced no relief, for loose stones rained down onto those below. After several days the party made it to a small saddle at 8,700 feet where they set up for the night, preparing for the summit bid.

"Most of the hard work of the ascent was over. With good weather we could be sure of reaching the top in two more days, for we could see our route now all the way and had just enough food and fuel left to go to the top and back on short rations." Keen had every reason to be hopeful.

But the air was unusually warm, and the men were afraid the weather would turn. They were right. "At 4:30 A.M. we wakened in a snowstorm. The wind had changed. The men recognized the signs of a three-day storm. We waited a while to be sure." But the men had spent years in Alaska and knew a blow when they saw one. "Silently, at 10:30, we turned down from what they had termed Keen Ridge."

Keen did not reach the summit of Mount Blackburn, but her party had made significant progress. "In mountain climbing, perhaps more than in any other sport, we appreciate each difficult point gained in proportion to what its attainment has cost us." On the personal side she found that exploring this formidable mountain exposed a new world, "a

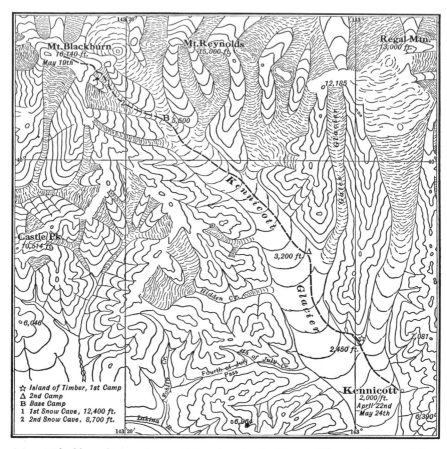

Mount Blackburn lies northwest of Kennicott in the Wrangell Range, from World's Work, *1913.*

world without limitations . . . a world in which I felt as if the bonds that held me to earth were loosened. . . . The struggles to achieve, the yearning to attain on the mountain, are they not symbolic of life? Life demands courage. We need strength to endure and to suffer. Is it not in itself worthwhile to climb if in so doing we lost all sense of fear?" Alaska gave Keen "a new spirit, a new optimism, a new standard of courage, and a new inspiration for life."

Keen was not to be thwarted by one unsuccessful attempt. Alaskan peaks took time, for they were uncharted territory. Two parties had turned back on Mount Saint Elias before the Duke of the Abruzzi had succeeded. During the winter Keen planned another bid, this time for the spring while the winter's snow still covered the glaciers and the going would be easier—or so she hoped.

Of her former party only John Barrett, who had driven the dog team, was able to rejoin her. The year before McClellan had done much of the organizational work, and now these tasks fell to Keen, who claimed they were almost as difficult as the physical side of the expedition. She hired seven men, including George Handy from Cordova, a German miner who had some experience climbing. She hired Handy "with some mistrust of my own judgment," perhaps because of her experience with the German "climber" who had deserted her the year before.

To Keen's dismay warm weather arrived a month earlier than normal. The party set off on April 22 with 2,000 pounds of food and gear. This time Keen used dogs with eight small sleds. She quickly realized she was too late to make the hoped-for easy ascent. The team members made their way 31 miles to the base of Mount Blackburn. The summit towered almost 11,000 feet above. They set up camp in the center of an amphitheater, where they hoped they would be safe from avalanches.

Avalanches became a greater danger as the party worked its way up to Crevice Camp. "The slides were a subject of constant study; we could calculate how to avoid them and had time to observe their movements before venturing in their path, and the men assured me that 'you could most generally always side-step them in time after you heard the first crack overhead'"—cool and dangerous advice from daredevil prospectors.

Conditions had changed from the previous summer, so the party had to work out a new course. Barrett announced that a route up a gully would work but would require a different strategy: "'It's all right if we go early,' he assured me. 'But I tell you,' and his face grew serious, 'We'll have to go light and rush for it; for that gulch is going to slide sometime, and if we keep a-traveling up and down it till we get all the stuff up, somebody's going to get killed. Just take food and what you have to have, and we men can sleep in the sun.'"

Barrett was proposing that Keen abandon the siege strategy, which involved relaying quantities of supplies up the mountain in successive stages. He was suggesting instead that they take the barest essentials to a higher camp and then bolt for the summit during a window in the weather. It was a bold idea, one that suited Alaska's mountains.

Keen and the men adopted the strategy and made it to the top of the gulch, only to find themselves trapped in snow caves by a three-day storm. Because they had chosen to travel light they had left their stove, bedding, and much of their food behind. The wait seemed endless. When they finally made it back to the lower camp, three men were so unnerved that they headed back to Kennicott; two more soon followed. Only Handy and Bill Lang stayed. Another storm dumped 20 feet of snow, halting Keen and her skeleton crew for almost two weeks.

Battered but determined, Keen, Lang, and Handy reclimbed the gulch and slogged toward the summit. Keen's account of the expedition, published in *World's Work* magazine six months later, fills in the details of the perilous endeavor (see excerpt from "First Up Mount Blackburn," following).

That same summer, after she had returned from Mount Blackburn, Keen embarked on a 300-mile trip by foot and boat through Alaska to the Yukon River; she was the first white woman to pass through the Skolai Pass. Handy accompanied her on this trip as well.

When Keen returned to the Lower 48, she met with acclaim. She was asked to give a presentation about her expedition to the prestigious American Alpine Club. Other explorers—including Vilhjalmur Stefansson, Sir Ernest Shackleton, Admiral Peary, and Belmore Browne (who had made several attempts on Mount McKinley)—also spoke. Keen, who was forty-one years old and 5 feet tall, must have provided a marked contrast to her male associates at the podium.

(Her route up Mount Blackburn has not been repeated. Climbers now fly onto a glacier on the north side and ascend a more gradual route with less danger of avalanche.)

Keen's experience on Mount Blackburn inextricably linked her with the Alaska frontier. In 1914 she returned to explore and map the Harvard Glacier in Prince William Sound, hiring the plucky Handy, a local sourdough, and a topographer from Boston. The Board of Geographic Names later named a section of the Chugach Mountains near the Harvard Glacier the Dora Keen Range.

Keen wrote and gave lectures about her expeditions. She wanted to reach out in particular to other women. "I believe more and more in the economic independence of women and in productive activities for them as for men. . . . I am eager to help the faint-hearted and that is my chief aim in writing and lecturing—to pass on the courage I have gained from my wonderful experiences."

Keen spoke from an unusual bully pulpit. The wealth and prominence of her parents, Dr. William W. and E. Corinna (Borden) Keen, placed them—and Keen—solidly in Philadelphia society. Keen had graduated from Bryn Mawr, a women's college, and had soon become involved in civic and volunteer efforts. "Where others filled their winters with dinners and cards, theatre and opera," a newspaper reported of Keen, "she was immersed in work for the Society for the Prevention of Cruelty to Children, or the American Society for Labor Legislation, or the Society for Organizing Charity, or in Suffragist circles." Keen's life choices were far from the norm of the Philadelphia elite.

In June 1916 Dora set out for Alaska with her sister Florence for an expedition in an entirely new arena. She married George Handy on July 8 in the little mining town of McCarthy, within sight of Mount Blackburn. After a two-month honeymoon trip in the wilderness, the couple moved to the green hills of West Hartford, Vermont, where they settled into country life and operated a farm. Dora later returned to Alaska to climb Mount Katmai in the Aleutian Range.

After sixteen years of marriage, when Keen was nearing her sixties, she and Handy were divorced. Dora remained on the farm in Vermont and launched a new career selling life insurance and annuities. She remained active and interested in the outside world. She traveled often and far, "all over the world excepting only Siberia and [the] interior of China." In her eighties, when she fled the cold Vermont winters, she found Florida "just filled with old people," so she went instead to South Africa, the Congo, Australia, New Guinea, Kenya, and Java. She maintained contact with the Appalachian Mountain Club, of which she had been an honored corresponding member since her Mount Blackburn climb.

In December 1962, at age ninety-one, Keen began a world tour. She headed straight for Alaska, which she had not visited since 1925. "I thirst for adventure, which I never get. People take too good care of me," she told a reporter for the *Anchorage Daily News* when she arrived there. She moved on to Tokyo and then to Hong Kong, where she died on January 31, 1963, never having quite quenched her thirst for adventure.

First Up Mt. Blackburn

We had reached 12,400 feet, and could now trace a route right up to the top. Indeed, the way seemed so clear that I estimated five to seven hours as all that would be needed to climb the 4,000 feet that remained, but it was impossible to proceed at once, for the snow had softened. It would be better to wait until daybreak.

Avalanches were pouring off the ridges below like loveliest bridal veil falls. We were too far up to hear or see any but the high ones. New mountains were in view, one far distant peak that seemed by its shape to be of volcanic origin, and by compass due east, 150 miles away, and perhaps 16,000 feet high. The panorama was one to linger over, but a chill breeze decided us to dig "igloos" or caves in the snow. The shovel flew and soon I "holed in" to mine, which reminded me of a sleeping-car berth—if only it had been as warm. "The smaller the warmer," they said, but it had the chill of the grave, and I had had to leave blanket and sleeping suit at Crevice Camp. Whenever I sat up or moved or arranged my hair, elbows and hair got full of snow. A flag pole marked each cave, lest someone step through the roof. The thermometer went down to 12 degrees and even with mitts and sweater on in my fur sleeping bag my feet were barely warm enough for me to sleep.

It was broad daylight when I awoke, to realize that I had not been called. Had the men then frozen to death? I wondered, as I hurried out to see. A snowstorm was raging. Stamping and tramping to keep warm, sitting on a snowshoe, or huddled over two candles trying to melt water and to warm it for tea or bouillon, I found five silent, cold, weary men. Unless we descended at once the trail would be covered and the rations for the summit depleted; but to venture down that fearful gulch in a blinding storm seemed to me out of the question. Moreover, I hoped that the weather would clear in time for us to go to the top and back without the added labor and danger of climbing down and up that gulch anew.

So we stayed, stayed three days, until the food was so nearly gone that there was no choice but to go down. Each day the storm had grown worse. Two feet of snow fell in 24 hours. By day I would lend my sleeping bag to two men at a time, who would take turns lying on it for two hours at a time, but to cover them I had only the maps of the now invisible glaciers. I had already lent both my extra sweaters. A snowshoe for a carpet kept our feet off the snow. I sat on my leather mitts, kept my hands in my armpits, and stamped my feet like the rest. At least numbers and candles made their cave warmer than mine. The next morning they dug me out three times and finally dug a small burrow off their cave for me. Outside it was warmer, but wet. They told me stories of their life in the wilderness, and always their talk was of timber and water and game. By the second day to climb out required four steps instead of two and inside it was darker.

On the 3rd of May we went into a howling, freezing, driving snowstorm to grope our way down the awful 3,500 feet that lay between us and more food.

"It don't look good to me," said my leader, as finally we found the top of the gulch. Without a word Mr. Handy took the lead, tested the snow, and started down. It was too cold to discuss the question. The slope was so steep and the snow so deep as to keep us wet to the waist half the time. Over crevasses and on down a now trailless path of danger, we seemed always to be just on the brink of some precipice or crevasse. We could not see 50 feet ahead, sometimes not 20—and yet they did not call it a blizzard. For just such a storm had I brought long bamboo flagpoles to mark the trail, but because they were troublesome in climbing, without asking me, the men had left them at Crevice Camp.

On went Mr. Handy, through all the hours never hesitating, except for the way when we could not see, never afraid, merely shouting back occasional warnings of crevasses or of steep ice underneath. For the latter Lang would anchor his ice ax and "snub us down," and the rope stood every test. It was as cool and brilliant a piece of leadership as I have ever seen. In four hours we were safely down that gulch to Crevice Camp.

We were back to the bedding, back to tents and a stove—but to wet bedding! The man at the camp had let the snow pile up on the tents and the bedding get against their wet walls. It was the last straw, wet bedding after three nights without any in a 16-degree snow cave!

The next morning it was still snowing. Mr. Barrett wanted to go for wood, the Finn and the two Swedes for good, and they left us, here at 8,700 feet, on the 4th of May.

"To wait for the haymaker"—as Lang called the sun—to dry the bedding was the only way, and that might mean rheumatism for life. Moreover, they thought that even when the storm ceased we should have to wait a week for that gulch either to slide or settle. Meanwhile the food would probably run short and the mountain grow too dangerous because of the rapidly advancing season. Thus they argued, and I would not ask anyone to go where he thought it unsafe. I had brought three extra men for the relaying only because I thought them needed to save time and I did not see how we could well go on without them, but Mr. Handy said, "Don't turn back unless you want to. We will get up without them." I had brought food and fuel for five weeks.

On the 9th of May a widely published Associated Press dispatch told of three men and two dogs that had "staggered into Kennicott, telling a thrilling tale," sent back—so the newspapers said—for more food and fuel. So they reported us *Marooned Near Top Mt. Blackburn, Facing Starvation.*

"Once more the Arctic silence closed about them," said the newspapers.

On Mt. Blanc people perish when overtaken by sudden storms, unless they can get to one of the refuge huts 4,000 feet apart. We had not even had tents, but we had dug caves in the snow, and had lived in them for three days with temperatures of 16 to 32 degrees and no stove.

Amid the yawning crevasses of Barrett Glacier, Mr. Handy, Lang, and I were all that were now left of the eight that had set out two weeks before for the summit of Mt. Blackburn. We had all the worst part to climb over again. We were only at 8,700 feet and it was already the 5th of May, but we were snowbound, and "May and June are the months of slides" had been my warning before I started.

Mr. Barrett had wished to see how Kolb and the dogs were faring and had gone down to the base camp the day before with the three men that were homeward bound. Today he was to come up again, bringing his tiny wood stove and the wood from the hardtack boxes. Mr. Handy and Lang went down to meet him. With Kolb and the dogs to help, Mr. Barrett was bringing up a big load of supplies on a sled as far as the crevasses.

We seemed safe on our mound, safely away from all walls and from all lines of breakage and flow. Suddenly a thundering roar made Lang step out. On the other side of the glacier, somewhere near our gulch, a great mass of ice had broken off and was falling. It had dropped 2,000 feet and came rolling onward like a great wave of surf and spray. It was flowing into the wide basin below us with a momentum which nothing could withstand. It was a mile away and on the side of the glacier where lay our trail to the base, and we were watching to see whether it would extend so far—when all of a sudden an icy, snow-laden gust told us to run for our lives to our dugout and, before we could get in, Lang and I were covered. We had got only a smart sprinkling, but the cloud of "spray" remained about five minutes or more, and when it had settled, so far as we could miss any mass on so huge and broken a glacier, it seemed as if a great area of ice had broken not from our gulch but from the ice cliffs above the rocks beside it.

It was snowing again and 26 degrees as we turned into our comfortable tents—the last time that we were to use them for seventeen days. The next morning the men were wet as they came from the crevasses with more packs; and the intervals without snow were too brief to dry anything.

Over a hot dinner we held a council of war. We had all been thinking: What if a big slide were to come from our side of the glacier, from above us? It could not fail to sweep us away, tents and all. Mr. Barrett decided to go down to the base camp, even if he had to cross the crevasses alone; but the chief part of the supplies was up now, and at the base we should be one day farther from the summit, so the rest of us preferred to stay and to make ourselves slide-proof in a snow cave. By tunneling into the steepest slope of our mound we would be safe, no matter how many slides went down over us, provided only that our roof were solid. Hence the cave must be small, just big enough for us to live in; and we three did live in it for nine days. It was about the size of a bathroom and half as high, 10 feet by 6, with 4 feet to stand in. Anything left out in the storm was lost in an hour, so everything had to be stowed away inside. In one end I managed to raise my tent just enough for me to crawl into at night and to keep my possessions dry.

The thermometer often went down to 21 degrees inside, but we could not have heat lest we weaken our snow roof or run out of oil, so between meals we would crawl into our sleeping bags. The hardest thing was to keep dry, for every time we went out we were in snow to our knees at the least and got wet all over, and the only way to dry anything was to sleep on it. Sometimes it would snow 3 feet in a day or a night. And yet, during the nine days in that snow cave we slept more, ate more, laughed more, and even washed more than all the rest of the time put together, and I think the thing I minded most about the entire expedition was that there were days when there was not enough water for me to brush my teeth.

One day Mr. Handy said, "I think that Barrett and Kolb will be wanting to turn back also; but I have spoken to Lang and he agrees that we two can get you to the top of the mountain alone, so don't you turn back, unless you want to."

On the 10th day of May, the tenth day of the storm (which had abated a little), for the first time it seemed safe to descend far enough to meet Mr. Barrett and Kolb. Mr. Barrett was anxious lest his wife worry and he lose his position by too long [an] absence. Both wished to go back; and with them would go the remaining dogs. Thus did we burn our bridges behind us; but Mr. Barrett was to return in two weeks to search for us if we had not then appeared. We turned and faced the wind to go back to our cave. The storm grew wild and we could barely follow our trail of two hours before.

For another three days the snow continued. We could do nothing but talk. Lang loved to repeat the German fairy stories of his childhood, "Snow White and Rose Red," and the rest, interlarding his philosophy of life. He was as simple as a child, although he was an old hunter and trapper from eastern Ontario. The wilds had no terrors for him. He "would just as lief be 1,500 miles away from the nearest man as not," and "could climb any mountain alone." He had neither received nor written a letter for fifteen years, but he "knew everyone in Alaska, pretty much" and he didn't want them to say, "Well, Bill, you couldn't make it, could you!" Alaska was getting too settled for him and he "guessed he'd be going to the Mackenzie River soon, where game was more plentiful-like."

Mr. Handy was the son of a German army officer. He was adventurous and daring by nature, but a disciplined soldier and always the first to subordinate his own interests to the good of the whole. He had been trained in a German technical school, had done his military service in southwest Africa, and had mined in South America, Mexico, California, and Alaska. He had even been a cowboy in Texas. For money he cared nothing, but he had enlisted for the summit of Mt. Blackburn and he always said, "Don't worry. We shall get to the top."

On the 13th of May, there came a lull in the storm, and at last we could venture to the base camp for some necessaries. As we were upward bound, the skies cleared. The thirteen-day snowstorm was over. Although it was 9:30 at night the sunset was only beginning to fade as we got back to our cave at Crevice Camp, and five hours later it was sunrise again as for the second time we were preparing to start up the mountain. Midsummer was upon us! Still, during the last seven days of the storm uniform temperatures had prevented all slides, the snow seemed to pack quickly, and we thought it safe to try our gulch at once.

Twenty feet or more of new snow now necessitated a long zigzag approach to the gulch on snowshoes instead of the former direct climb up across the basin at its foot. To sound and break the trail as they relayed two packs and to test the gulch was all that could be done that day. They could go faster without me, and their parting words were, "If we don't come back, do you think you can get home alone?" and my reply, "I'll try." In half an hour I saw them disappear. Was it forever, or were they behind that hill? They had seemed to be making straight for the place where, just as they started, a great pinnacle of ice had fallen from 2,000 feet above. At last I saw them again, far above, and this time in the path of slides from that cliff next [to] our gulch. "Well," Lang had said, "if we're killed we'll get our names in the papers, anyhow."

They thought the gulch safe, but the perpetual daylight in the Northern summer had come. Henceforth daytime travel would be unsafe and the nights might prove too short and warm for the freezing which alone prevented slides and gave a crust. At 10 that night, 11, midnight, still there was no crust. Although I sank to my hips as I put on my snowshoes, we could wait no longer.

At dawn on the 15th of May, for the second time we lost sight of Crevice Camp, once again to strain every nerve to get up that gulch before the slides could begin. Once more we had left tents and stove behind, but this time I had insisted that the men take their bedding. So there were five loads for two men, there was no relay party, and the deep new snow would be certain to double the time; and the hours of safe travel had dwindled to the brief period of a dusk and dawn that could hardly be told apart. Indeed, all the conditions were changed, and the ascent would now be twice as hard as before the storm. The difficulties were as great or greater than the previous August when we had given up this route as too dangerous, but I knew my men and I trusted their judgment and ability.

The night was clear and I could drink in the beauty of it all while the men rested from their heavy packs. Lang would roll his pack off, exclaiming, "There, you've been lying on me long enough! It's my turn to lie on you awhile."

At 2 o'clock in the morning we were under the treacherous rock cliffs and amid huge snowballs, telltales of slides. Lang pointed to the overhanging upper lip of a big crevasse beside us now drifted half full of snow, saying, "There, that's the kind of a place to get in if a slide comes." Hardly had he spoken when there was a loud report overhead as of an explosion, and we looked up to see ice cliffs descending upon us. "Come here!" cried Lang from behind, and as we were roped we had to, although the quickest way to safety lay ahead. As I turned, the tails of my snowshoes caught and I upset. Two of us had yet to cross a narrow slanting ledge of ice overhanging a crevasse, but somehow we reached shelter just in time to be halfway under as the slide came on. As we crouched, "Dig in your ice pick!" were the last words I heard. A moment and it had passed, and for a second time we had only 2 inches of snow all over us, for an intervening gully had received most of the slide. The route the men had chosen *was* a safe one.

Once at the foot of the gulch, despite the softness of the snow the angle necessitated creepers. The sun was already hot as at 3:15 we began the ascent of that 3,000-foot nightmare gulch. To climb the first 150 feet I had to take hold of the rope, for it was 76 degrees and all ice underneath, but Mr. Handy had not even chopped steps as he had taken the rope up to anchor it. The steeper the slope the better he liked it. He did not call the zigzag method climbing. He was never afraid, yet he never led us into danger. Until 9 o'clock we would be safe even here, and by that hour surely we hoped to be in our cave above the wall. A deep groove like a toboggan slide told where something had come down, and I was glad when the last pack and the last man were above instead of beside it.

Hauling seemed the quickest and easiest way for two men to get five packs up so steep a gulch. To a "sleigh" or "buggy," as he called it, made from two shoes, Lang would tie two packs at a time, and around an anchored ice ax Mr. Handy would "line them" up 80 feet at a time. I helped to haul or broke trail ahead. I had to choose the steepest places in order that the sled might slide; yet, work as we would, by 5 o'clock in the morning, it would no longer slide either up or down. Trail breaking had become such deep, steep work that I was pressing first one knee and then the other ahead and still rising only 3 inches at a time. By 7 o'clock the snow was so soft and the slope so steep that bits of snow, "snowballs," were rolling down on us—warning of slides to follow. We were exhausting ourselves and still we were making no progress. It was time to be out of such a place, and yet we could not hope to get up the remaining 1,200 feet to our cave before the slides should begin. We were only two-thirds of the way up the gulch, and I could not see even a safe place to camp. Indeed, to look up was appalling, for to the right and left beetling ice cliffs loomed threateningly overhead. It was the only time when I felt that we were really in grave danger and saw no way out of it; but Lang had more experience than I. "Why," he said, "we can camp 'most anywhere as far as that goes," and he pointed to the "shelter" of one ice mount after another as a good campsite! Under an eyelid of ice, as it were, deep in the recesses of a snow-filled ice cave, we spread our bedding and awaited the night. A great crack right across our roof warned us away from its edge. A fringe of icicles, like eyelashes, dropped merrily—so long as the sun was on them—giving us water.

We were safe from anything that might come, and yet I could not sleep for the thunder of the many slides on every side. None came near us until midday, when twice the deep rolling of falling ice made me sit up with a start just as a great mass went sweeping by. They were the most awe-inspiring sight that I have ever seen, so wonderful, so thrilling to watch, that I wished I did not need sleep. They passed so close that it was as if the American Falls at Niagara were suddenly overwhelming us. It was the most exciting day of the entire ascent. Still nothing came over us, and at 3:30 in the afternoon I got up. The higher we rose the fewer the slides— but on the descent the opposite would be true. I looked down and there at the foot of our gulch, 2,000 feet below, lay the fragments of a great slide spread out like a fan. It had gone down since we had come up just there a few hours before. It was the third big slide we had escaped, and again it was judgment more than good fortune that had saved us. We had been there at an hour that was safe.

We had reached 11,000 feet, and still there was no crust as again we started upward at 10 o'clock in the evening, none until the cold breeze of dawn found us on a glazed slope where a crust left no foothold. Just as we seemed to have reached the top of the gulch bad crevasses caused delay. It grew late and we looked upward anxiously. Weary from the lack of food we had to stop to eat in none too safe a place. At the top, steps had to be chopped and when at length we were up, utterly weary from the disheartening struggle in knee-deep snow, the most we could do was to crawl into a shaded shelter as far as possible from the great ice wall above. For the lack of a relay party and because of the advance in the season, it had taken thirteen hours to get merely food, bedding, and essential outfit up 1,000 feet.

In the seventeen days since we had dug out our first cave above this wall all had changed. New blocks had parted from it. The great 60-foot ice needles under which we had once hurried had fallen. Landmarks were gone and just to find the way up 200 feet again to our "igloo" and to dig it out took all that night. Only by the bare tip of a bamboo pole did we discover it. It had become a burrow and to descend into it required twelve steps. We had been four days regaining the 3,500 feet which we had before climbed in as many hours. For the second time we had reached 12,400 feet. Between 10,000 and 12,500 feet what appeared to be a volcanic ash discolored the snow.

At 9 o'clock in the evening it seemed as if we should really reach the summit that night. The slope was easier, slides were improbable so high up, and although snowshoes were still required, moccasins had replaced rubber shoe-packs lest our feet freeze. We had only 4,000 feet to go, and to avoid further relaying the men decided to leave their bedding.

At midnight the wind pierced us as we exchanged snowshoes for creepers, only to need the snowshoes again when they were far behind. For an hour we were wallowing to our knees. Then a thin crust made us take to all fours, and still we broke through. For the breakfast halt we sought shelter but found none, until Lang dug a third cave. The distance had been considerable and although it was 3 o'clock in the morning we had reached only 14,000 feet.

An ocean of billowy clouds covered Kennicott Glacier. The earth lay hidden from view and only the mountaintops appeared as the tints of the dawn added the last touch to the most superb view of my life. As we watched, the peaks took fire and in a moment over the snowy spires of Mt. Reynolds the sun crept forth.

Although at 3:30 the thermometer showed only 6 degrees, before we could start again trail breaking had become so arduous that it seemed best to wait for the shadows. With makeshift coverings and moving as the sun moved we slept a little. At 5 o'clock in the evening Lang started up the last 2,000 feet. He was ploughing to his knees and the slope had become steep enough for him to zigzag.

At 15,000 feet our packs made us begin to feel the altitude a little. Because of the moccasins my creepers refused to say firm, and to rebind them was a long, cold process. We were not getting up very fast, but it was no place for a slip. At 9 o'clock at night we saw Lang depositing my bedding above, at the only level spot. Presently we also would be there with the shovel to dig a last cave, the fourth—for a brief rest. The next moment he was running down, pausing as he passed only long enough to say that he felt a little sick and, since he "had no bet on getting to the top," he thought he would go down to his bedding and wait. After twenty-seven days of misery he had turned down within 500 feet of the top. Of the seven men in our party that had started, one alone remained.

It was zero at midnight. Even at sunrise it was only 3 degrees. To thaw a tin of salmon over two candles took an hour. The final slope was steep and slippery, and even so high there were holes. We were a full hour climbing it, and when at length we thought the summit attained, we found that it was a half mile plateau on which a half hour's wandering and use of the level were necessary in order to determine the highest point. Indeed, at first a twin summit at least 2 miles away to the northwest appeared the higher one. A long snow saddle connected them. Finally, however, at the northeast edge of the southeast summit we seemed to be standing on the top of Mt. Blackburn, all that were left of us, two of eight. It was 8:30 in the morning and the 19th of May. Even a temperature of 6 degrees and an ice gale from which there was no shelter failed to mar the satisfaction of achievement in the accomplishment of a difficult task. It had taken four weeks.

There was nothing to impair a view upon which our eyes were the first that had ever looked and the panorama seemed limited only by the haze of distance as we gazed a full 200 miles on every side. Probably nowhere except in Alaska, not even in the Himalayas, could mortal man attain to the centre of so vast and imposing a stretch of unbroken snow over great glaciers and high snow peaks. Literally hundreds of them rose above the line of perpetual snow. The limited snow areas of the Alps, the Canadian Rocky Mountains, even the high Andes, faded into insignificance in my memory. We were in the very midst of the Wrangell Mountains, of which Mt. Blackburn was within 60 feet of the highest. All were snow peaks, and at least six of them rose above 12,000 feet, more than 9,000 feet above the snowline. Each could be plainly distinguished and identified, Mt. Sanford, the highest,

Mt. Drum, Mt. Jarvis, and Mt. Wrangell, from the volcanic cone of which a faint column of white smoke was rising lazily. Although many miles away, no doubt this was the source of the fragments of burnt-out granite with which our plateau was strewn.

Between us and Mt. Jarvis to the north lay the immense unbroken snow field of the Nabesna Glacier. It was seemingly three times as extensive as the great Kennicott Glacier upon which it had taken us five days to come. From Mt. Blackburn's summit two precipitous glaciers descended to it, contradicting my prediction of an easy northeast slope. On the west side, if anywhere, would lie the better route. We had hoped to explore all sides of our peak, but its area, the wind, the fatigue of climbing up again whenever we went down, and the long descent we had yet to make prevented [us from doing so].

With aching hands and in wind-hardened snow—for lack of any rock at all—we planted and guyed the bamboo flagpole which we had dragged up, burying beneath it a brief record of the first ascent of this great 16,140-foot sub-arctic peak.

After four hours and a half, relief from the cold wind became imperative and we turned downward to rejoin Lang below.

With crevasses opening all but under us as we waited for snow bridges to harden, three days of anxious work brought us to the base, and two days more to Kennicott on the 24th of May.

Because of the latitude, to climb up and down 11,000 feet of snow and ice had required twenty-six days. After thirty-three days entirely on snow and ice, of which twenty-two nights had been spent without tents and ten days without fuel, we were back—back to wood and water, to green grass and spring flowers, to civilization and friends.

Alaskan mountaineering is so new that the whole undertaking had been an experiment. Latitude and location are as important as altitude in determining the difficulty of a mountain ascent, and chiefly because of its latitude the problems of Alaskan mountaineering are new and wholly different from those of other regions. It is like Arctic exploration. Elsewhere difficulties of approach may be as great, the time required as long, and altitudes higher, but nowhere else is the time on snow and ice so long. Nowhere else does one have to climb 14,000 feet above the snowline, as on Mt. Blackburn, or even 17,000 feet, as on Mt. McKinley, which is only 20,300 feet high. Nowhere but in Alaska is the mountaineer obliged to be entirely on snow and ice and to choose between safety at the price of almost unendurable cold, or soft snow and avalanches, according as he goes early or late in the only season at which an ascent can be attempted. Not even in the Himalayas are the glaciers so extensive.

On Mt. Blackburn and Mt. McKinley, the discoverer of the North Pole has said, the problem of Alaskan mountaineering has been solved. The Parker-Browne expeditions and mine have proved that the secret of success lies in going early and in using dogs. Our 1911 expedition had been the first to use dogs on a mountain and the one here recounted was the first to succeed without Swiss guides, the first to live in snow caves, the first to make a prolonged night ascent, the first to succeed on an avalanche-swept southeast side, and the only Alaskan ascent in which a woman had taken part— to the credit of the men be it said. We succeeded because one man cared to succeed.

*Grace Gallatin Seton was equally at home in society cir-
cles and the wilderness, from* Good Housekeeping, *1912.*

5

A TENDERFOOT NO LONGER
Grace Gallatin Seton
(1872–1959)

> *I have felt the charm of the glorious*
> *freedom, the quick rushing blood,*
> *the bounding motion, of the wild life,*
> *the joy of the living and of the doing, of*
> *the mountain and the plain; I have*
> *learned to know and feel some, at least,*
> *of the secrets of the Wild Ones. In short,*
> *though I am still a woman and may*
> *be tender, I am a Woman Tenderfoot*
> *no longer.*

 **Unlike many of the women** in this book, Grace Gal-
latin did not seek out the rigors of the wilderness on her own.
She was born in California on January 28, 1872, to Albert Gallatin and Clemenzia (Rhodes) Gallatin, but she moved to New
York City after her mother's divorce and remarriage. Her mother and
stepfather were part of a glittering social and cultural scene.

Grace was privately educated. She later studied bookmaking and printing and began writing articles about cultural affairs. In 1894 she and her mother sailed for Paris so she could study the arts. On the way they met a tall man with animated dark eyes and skin burnished a deep copper by the sun. Ernest Thompson Seton was a naturalist, artist, and writer from Canada who was headed to Paris to refine his skills and seek his fortune.

Seton was kind to the women, helping them settle in when they reached France. Grace continued writing—now for French and English as well as U.S. audiences—and became Seton's assistant, helping him with the text of his current book. It was little wonder that they fell in love. He was handsome and ambitious; she was feisty, attractive, and wealthy. They were married in 1896 in New York City.

Grace turned her efforts to furthering her husband's career, teaming up with her mother to arrange for an exhibit of his work in New York and then accompanying him on a wildlife-viewing trip out West. They went first to a remote ranch on the Green River, then on to Yellowstone Park, to the Crow Reservation on the Little Bighorn River in Montana, and to a ranch in North Dakota.

Although Grace was a complete tenderfoot, used to creature comforts like a tub bath and a comfortable bed, she adapted quickly to the rough demands of the terrain. Her trail-hardened husband praised her: "As a camper she was a great success, never grumbled at hardship, or scolded anyone. She . . . met all kinds of danger with unflinching nerve; was always calm and clear-headed, no matter what the stance."

The couple spent ensuing summers in the West, where Ernest studied and drew wildlife. When they were not traveling, Ernest worked on a series of books and carried out a vigorous lecture schedule, and Grace took over the management of his publications. She edited them, did the general layout, and designed covers and title pages. Her keen literary sense was invaluable to Ernest's success.

This literary sense was valuable to her, too. *A Woman Tenderfoot* was published in 1900 in England and in 1905 in the United States. In the book Seton presents herself as "the woman-who-goes-hunting-with-her-husband." In some ways it is her least mature writing. These are her first ventures into the wilderness, and she is obviously a young urban wife devoted to her more experienced husband.

But *A Woman Tenderfoot* (see excerpts, following) is also a primer for women's independence. Seton gives practical advice: Don't ride sidesaddle; make sure a camp cook has been hired. She presents her design for a riding outfit that allows freedom of movement on and off a horse. She suggests equipment and clothing that will make camp life more comfortable. And although she shares the misery and mishaps that are part of outdoor life, she also shows her readers how they, too, can succeed.

Seton learns how to handle her horse, a rifle, and her fear. She discovers that she can be tough when circumstances warrant and still appreciate the wonder and beauty of the places around her. In a wonderful vignette about getting lost and then found, she concludes, "Always regulate your fears according to the situation, and then you will not go into the valley of the shadow of death, when you are only lost in the mountains." Her husband introduced her to the outdoors, but it was her spirit alone that allowed her to embrace the wilderness. These were formative times for Seton. She returned from each trip West, less the pampered sophisticate of her youth and more the confident adventurer. These experiences laid the foundation for her growing independence from her husband and her career as a writer, explorer, and advocate for women's rights.

After seven years of marriage Seton gave birth to Ann, called Anya. Like other well-to-do mothers, Seton left her daughter in the hands of a governess. Grace and Ernest spent a month canoeing on the Ottawa River the year Anya was born, but Grace subsequently accompanied Ernest on his wilderness tours less often. In 1906 she finished her second book, *Nimrod's Wife*, which covered her wilderness outings since *A Woman Tenderfoot*. When Ernest set off on an Arctic canoe trip in 1907, Grace stayed home to publicize her book. She also established the Pen

Seton designed this riding suit for women to wear when riding astride, from her book A Woman Tenderfoot.

and Brush Club and served as vice president of the Connecticut Woman's Suffrage Association.

Whereas Grace had at one time devoted herself to Ernest's career, now she was busy with her own. Moreover, Ernest was becoming more conservative, believing in a natural distribution of duties (with women bearing and rearing children and men providing for the family). Although he believed in general that women should not be subservient to men, he resented Grace's independence. This dissension threaded through their marital problems for years to come.

"The Feminine Charm of the Woman Militant," a 1912 article in *Good Housekeeping* that featured Seton and other suffragists, offers an interesting look at the contrasts in Grace's life. Although she "gave all her time to reform work," she was still Mrs. Ernest Thompson Seton—a woman who scrupulously superintended the country estate, tended to a stream of visitors, kept the "domestic wheels moving smoothly and noiselessly," and oversaw a beautiful perennial garden. "With all her talents Mrs. Seton is perhaps most proud of her ability to invent new dishes and to design new gowns," wrote the interviewer. This was the same woman who rode horseback in the mountains and canoed on the Ottawa River and whose plan for the Camp Fire Girls was rejected because it called for developing leadership rather than homemaking skills. A later article about Seton reveals these same incongruities:

> Although Mrs. Seton's bearing in the drawing room gives one the impression of a sheltered, beautifully groomed hostess and seems to contradict her adventurous spirit, in her sparkling blue eyes one can see the mischief-loving, determined, highly intelligent being which is her true character. She loves danger and deliberately courts it in her arduous pursuit of first-hand knowledge from the untamed tribes of hidden lands.

Between 1910 and 1920 Seton continued to work for suffrage, eventually serving as president of the Connecticut association. She was appalled to learn that even if women gained the vote she would not be allowed to exercise her right because her husband retained his British citizenship. During World War I Seton answered the call of patriotism by raising money to create a motor unit—with women drivers—that did relief work just behind the lines in France. Seton directed this unit for two years.

In the 1920s and 1930s Seton satisfied her yearning for adventure through a series of trips—without Ernest—to Egypt, China, Japan, Africa, India, South America, and Southeast Asia. (She had long since stopped accompanying her husband on his wildlife tours.) Armed with letters of introduction to key political and social players, she was able to explore the far corners of each country she visited. Often, she was the only woman on the expedition. Seton was genuinely curious about the customs, politics, and social structure of the areas she visited. She talked with women—those who had influence and those who did not—about their position in the country and their dreams for the future. From these adventures she wrote first-person accounts of far-off lands: *A Woman Tenderfoot in Egypt* (1923), *Chinese Lanterns* (1924), "Yes, Lady Saheb": *A Woman's Adventurings with Mysterious India* (1925), *Magic Waters* (about South America, 1933), and *Poison Arrows* (about Southeast Asia, 1938).

In *Poison Arrows* she describes a moment fraught with peril when her party encountered a band of sixty warriors armed with poison-tipped arrows. Seton got off her elephant and—alone—approached the chief. She extended her hand and smiled. She was the first white woman he had ever seen; the fate of her entire party rested on that smile. The chief accepted her peaceful gesture. He subsequently called her the "Far Off Smile Woman."

Seton's books were well received, especially in women's circles. The League of American Penwomen chose "Yes, Lady Saheb" as the best-written book of 1925, and a Century of Progress committee selected *A Woman Tenderfoot in Egypt* as one of the best one-hundred books written by an American woman in the century preceding 1933.

In the course of her work, Seton established herself as a writer, explorer, lecturer, and organizer.

During these travels Seton's marriage was on a long downhill slide. She and Ernest coexisted by not seeing each other for extended periods. There were accusations of infidelity on both sides. Ernest began traveling with his secretary. Despite attempts at reconciliation, Grace and Ernest were divorced in 1935. Although Grace had many subsequent suitors, she never remarried. Ernest married his secretary, who was thirty years his junior, the day after the divorce.

Both before and after the divorce, Seton was active in several women's organizations. She was one of eight charter members of the Society of Woman Geographers (an organization Annie Peck joined in 1928). She served as president of the National League of Pen Women and was a frequent delegate to women's conventions around the world. She solicited books for and established a unique three thousand–volume collection called the Biblioteca Femina, now housed at the Northwestern University Library. The collection calls attention to the contributions of women writers worldwide and honors their often unrecognized work.

Despite numerous separations during Anya's younger years, Seton and her daughter became close and began living together in 1930, after Anya's second divorce. They remained together until Grace's death on March 19, 1959, in Palm Beach.

Seton was eighty-seven when she left a world much changed from the one into which she had been born. She believed in women's rights at an early age and worked on the front lines to secure the right to vote. Wealth allowed her to choose her own way. She was not financially dependent on her husband; to the contrary, in the early years of their marriage he was dependent on her.

As wives often did at the time and still do now, Seton helped her husband further his career. By accompanying him on his wilderness travels she discovered a new part of herself, developing a love of adventure that would last throughout her life. In time, when she turned to her own career and worked for the principles she held dear, Ernest became less and less central.

Unlike Dora Keen, who was born into and rejected society life, Seton excelled in both the social arena and the wilderness. Whereas Keen was content to adjourn to a quiet Vermont farm, Seton pushed for change in the status of women. And whereas Annie Peck wrote *The Apex of America* to prove what she had done to an audience of critics, Seton showed her mettle during her first trips out West and then set out to encourage women to fulfill their dreams. By fulfilling her own dreams—and satisfying her own quest for adventure—she provided a strong role model for fellow seekers.

A Woman Tenderfoot
Outfit and Advice for the Woman-Who-Goes-Hunting-with-Her-Husband

Is it really so that most women say no to camp life because they are afraid of being uncomfortable and looking unbeautiful? There is no reason why a woman should make a freak of herself even if she is going to rough it; as a matter of fact I do not rough it, I go for enjoyment and leave out all possible discomforts. There is no reason why a woman should be more uncomfortable out in the mountains, with the wild west wind for companion and the big blue sky for a roof, than sitting in a 10 by 12 whitewashed bedroom of the summer hotel variety, with the tin roof to keep out what air might be passing. A possible mosquito or gnat in the mountains is no more irritating than the objectionable personality that is sure to be forced upon you every hour at the summer hotel. The usual walk, the usual drive, the usual hop, the usual novel, the usual scandal—in a word, the continual consciousness of self as related to dress, to manners, to position, which the gregarious living of a hotel enforces—are all right enough once in a while; but do you not get enough of such life in the winter to last for all the year?

Is one never to forget that it is not proper to wear gold beads with crape? Understand, I am not to be set down as having any charity for the ignoramus who would wear that combination, but I wish to record the fact that there are times, under the spell of the West, when I simply do not *care* whether there are such things as gold beads and crape; when the whole business of city life, the music, arts, drama, the pleasant friends, equally with the platitudes of things and people you care not about—civilization, in a word—when all these fade away from my thoughts as far as geographically they are, and in their place comes the joy of being at least a healthy, if not an intelligent, animal. It is a pleasure to eat when the time comes around, a good old-fashioned pleasure, and you need no dainty serving to tempt you. It is another pleasure to use your muscles, to buffet with the elements, to endure long hours of riding, to run where walking would do, to jump an obstacle instead of going around it, to return, physically at least, to your pinafore days when you played with your brother Willie. Red blood means a rose-colored world. Did you feel like that last summer at Newport or Narragansett?

So enough; come with me and learn how to be healthy and robust.

Of course one must have clothes and personal comforts, so, while we are still in the city humor, let us order a habit suitable for riding astride. Whipcord, or a closely woven homespun, in some shade of grayish brown that harmonizes with the landscape, is best. Corduroy is pretty, if you like it, but rather clumsy. Denham will do, but it wrinkles and becomes untidy. Indeed it has been my experience that it is economy to buy the best quality of cloth you can afford, for then the garment always keeps its shape, even after hard wear, and can be cleaned and made ready for another year, and another, and another. You will need it, never fear. Once you have opened your ears, "the Red Gods" will not cease to "call for you."

In western life you are on and off your horse at the change of a thought. Your horse is not an animate exercise maker that John brings around for a couple of hours each morning; he is your companion, and shares the vicissitudes of your life. You even consult him on occasion, especially on matters relating to the road. Therefore your costume must look equally well on and off the horse. In meeting this requirement, my woes were many. I struggled valiantly with everything in the market, and finally, from five varieties of divided skirts and bloomers, the following practical and becoming habit was evolved.

I speak thus modestly, as there is now a trail of patterns of this habit from the Atlantic to the Pacific Coast. Wherever it goes, it makes converts, especially among the wives of army officers at the various western posts where we have been—for the majority of women in the West, and I nearly said all the sensible ones, now ride astride.

When off the horse, there is nothing about this habit to distinguish it from any trim golf suit, with the stitching up the left front which is now so popular. When on the horse, it looks, as someone phrased it, as though one were riding sidesaddle on both sides. This is accomplished by having the fronts of the skirt double, free nearly to the waist, and, when off the horse, fastened by patent hooks. The back seam is also open, faced for several inches, stitched and closed by patent fasteners. Snug bloomers of the same material are worn underneath. The simplicity of this habit is its chief charm; there is no superfluous material to sit upon—oh, the torture of wrinkled cloth in the divided skirt!—and it does not fly up even in a strong wind, if one knows how to ride. The skirt is 4 inches from the ground—it should not bell much on the sides—and about 3 and a half yards at the bottom, which is finished with a five-stitched hem. . . .

I had a man's saddle, with a narrow tree and high pommel and cantle, such as is used out West, and as I had not ridden a horse since the hazy days of my infancy, I got on the huge creature's back with everything to learn. Fear enveloped me as in a cloud during my first ride, and the possibilities of the little cow pony they put me on seemed more awe inspiring than those of a locomotive. But I had been reading Professor William James and acquired from him the idea (I hope I do not malign him) that the accomplishment of a thing depends largely upon one's mental attitude, and this was mine all nicely taken—in New York:—

"This thing has been done before, and done well. Good; then I can do it, and *enjoy* it too."

I particularly insisted upon the latter clause—in the East. This formula is applicable in any situation. I never should have gotten through my western experiences without it, and I advise you, my dear woman-who-goes-hunting-with-her-husband, to take a large stock of it made up and ready for use. There is one other rule for your conduct, if you want to be a success: think what you like, but unless it is pleasant, *don't say it.*

Is it better to ride astride? I will not carry the battle-ground into the East, although even here I have my opinion; but in the West, in the mountains, there can be no question that it is the *only way*. . . . A woman at best is physically handicapped when roughing it with husband or brother. Then why increase that handicap by wearing trailing skirts that catch on every log and bramble, and which demand the services of at least one hand to hold up (fortunately this battle is already won), and by choosing to ride sidesaddle, thus making it twice as difficult to mount and dismount by yourself, which in fact compels you to seek the assistance of a log, or stone, or a friendly hand for a lift? Western riding is not Central Park riding, nor is it Rotten Row riding. The cowboy's, or military, seat is much simpler and easier for both man and beast than the park seat—though, of course, less stylish. That is the glory of it; you can go galloping over the prairie and uplands with never a thought that the trot is more proper, and your course, untrammelled by fenced-in roads, is straight to the setting sun or to yonder butte. And if you want a spice of danger, it is there, sometimes more than you want, in the presence of badger and gopher holes, to step into which while at high speed may mean a broken leg for your horse, perhaps a broken neck for yourself. . . .

Besides being unable to mount and dismount without assistance it is very difficult to get sidesaddle broken horses, and it usually means a horse so broken in health and spirits that he does not care what is being strapped on his back and dangling on one side of him only. And to be on such an animal means that you are on the worst mount of the outfit, and I am sure that it requires little imagination on anyone's part to know therein lies misery. Oh! the weariness of being the weakest of the party and the worst mounted—to be always at the trail end of the line, never to be able to keep up with the saddle horses when they start off for a canter, to expend your stock of vitality, which you should husband for larger matters, in urging your beast by voice and quirt to further exertion! Never place yourself in such a position. The former you cannot help, but you can lessen it by making use of such aids to greater independence as wearing short skirts and riding astride, and having at least as good a horse as there is in the outfit. Then you will get the pleasure from your outing that you have the right to expect—that is, if you adhere to one other bit of advice, or rather two.

The first is: See that your camping trip is provided [with] a man cook.

I wish that I could put a charm over the next few words so that only the woman reader could understand, but as I cannot I must repeat boldly: Dear woman-who-goes-hunting-with-her-husband, be sure that you have it understood that you do no cooking, or dishwashing. I think that the reason women so often dislike camping out is because the only really disagreeable part of it is left to them as a matter of course. Cooking out-of-doors at best is trying, and certainly you cannot be carefree, camp life's greatest charm, when you have on your mind the boiling of prunes and beans, or when the tears are starting from your smoke-inflamed eyes as you broil the elk steak for dinner. No, indeed! See that your guide or your horse wrangler knows how to cook, and expects to do it. He is used to it, and, anyway, is paid for it. He is earning his living, you are taking a vacation.

Now for the second advice, which is a codicil to the above: in return for not having to potter with the food and tinware, *never complain about it.* Eat everything that is set before you, shut your eyes to possible dirt, or, if you cannot, leave the particular horror in question untouched, but without comment. Perhaps in desperation you may assume the role of cook yourself. Oh, foolish woman, if you do, you only exchange your woes for worse ones.

The First Plunge of the Woman Tenderfoot

First, it becomes necessary to confide in you. Fear is a very wicked companion who, since nursery days, had troubled me very little; but when I arrived out West, he was

GRACE GALLATIN SETON

waiting for me, and, so that I need never be without him, he divided himself into a band of little imps.

Each imp had a special duty, and never left me until he had been crushed in silent but terrible combat. There was the imp who did not like to be alone in the mountains and the imp who was sure he was going to be lost in those wildernesses, and the imp who quaked at the sight of a gun, and the imp who danced a mad fierce dance when on a horse. All these had been conquered, or at least partially reduced to subjection, but the imp who sat on the saddle pommel when there was a ditch or stream to be jumped had hitherto obliged me to dismount and get over the space on foot.

This morning, when we came to a nasty boggy place, with several small water cuts running through it, I obeyed the imp with reluctance. Well, we got over it—Blondey, the imp, and I—with nothing worse than wet feet and shattered nerves.

I attempted to mount, and had one foot in the stirrup and one hand on the pommel, when Blondey started. Like the girl in the song, I could not get up, I could not get down, and although I had hold of the reins, I had no free hand to pull them in tighter, and you may be sure the imp did not help me. Blondey, realizing there was something wrong, broke into a wild gallop across country, but I clung on, expecting every moment the saddle would turn, until I got my foot clear from the stirrup. Then I let go just as Blondey was gathering himself together for another ditch.

I was stunned, but escaped any serious hurt. Nimrod [Ernest] was a great deal more undone than I. He had not dared to go fast for fear of making Blondey go faster, and he now came rushing up, with the fear of death upon his face and the most dreadful words on his lips.

Although a good deal shaken, I began to laugh, the combination was so incongruous. Nimrod rarely swears, and was now quite unconscious what his tongue was doing. Upon being assured that all was well, he started after Blondey and soon brought him back to me; but while he was gone the imp and I had mortal combat.

I did up my hair, rearranged my habit, and, rejecting Nimrod's offer of his quieter horse, remounted Blondey. We all jumped the next ditch, but the shock was too much for the imp in his weakened condition; he tumbled off the pommel, and I have never seen him since.

What I Know About Wahb of the Bighorn Basin

It was an endless day of freezing in the saddle, and of snow showers in one's face from the overladen branches. I was frightfully cold and miserable. Every minute seemed the last I could endure without screeching. But still our host pushed on. It was necessary to get near enough to the top of the Continental Divide so that we could cross it the next day. It began to grow dark about three o'clock; the storm increased. I kept saying over and over to myself what I was determined I should not say out loud:

"Oh, please stop and make camp! I cannot stay in this saddle another minute. My left foot is frozen. I know it is, and the saddle cramp is unbearable. I am so hungry, so cold, so exhausted; oh, please stop!" Then, having wailed this out under my breath, I would answer it harshly: "You little fool, stop your whimpering. The others are made of flesh and blood too. We should be snowbound if we stopped here. Don't be a crybaby. There is lots of good stuff in you yet. This only seems terrible because you are not used to it, so brace up."

Then I would even smile at Nimrod who kept keen watch on me, or wave my hand at the host, who was in front.

This appearance of unconcern helped me for a few seconds, and then I would begin the weary round: "Oh, my foot, my back, my head; I cannot endure it another moment; I can't, I can't." Yet all the while knowing that I could and would. Thus I fought through the afternoon, and at last became just a numb thing on the horse with but one thought, "I can and will do it." So at last when the order came to camp in 4 feet of snow 10,000 feet above the sea, with the wind and snow blowing a high gale, I just drew rein and sat there on my tired beast.

We disturbed a band of mountain sheep that got over the deep snow with incredible swiftness. It was my first view of these animals, but it aroused no enthusiasm in me, only a vague wonder that they seemed to be enjoying themselves. Finally Nimrod came and pulled me off, I was too stiff and numb to get down myself. Then I found that the snow was so deep I could not go 4 feet. Not to be able to move about seemed to me the end of all things. I simply dropped in the snow—it was impossible to ever be warm and happy again—and prepared at last to weep.

But I looked around first—Nimrod was coaxing a pack animal through the snow to a comparatively level place where our tent and bed things could be placed. The host was shoveling a pathway between me and the spot where the cook was coaxing a fire. The horsewrangler was unpacking the horses alone (so that I might have a fire the sooner). They were all grim—doubtless as weary as I—but they were all working for my ultimate comfort, while I was about to repay them by sitting in the snow and weeping. I pictured them in four separate heaps in the snow, all weeping. This was too much; I did not weep. Instead by great effort I managed to get my horse near the fire, and after thawing out a moment unsaddled the tired animal, who galloped off gladly to join his comrades, and thus I became once more a unit in the economic force.

The Last Word

Now this is the end. It is three years since I first became a woman-who-goes-hunting-with-her-husband. I have lived on jerked deer and alkali water, and bathed in dark-eyed pools, nestling among vast pines where none but the four-footed had been before. I have been sung asleep a hundred times by the coyotes' evening lullaby, have felt the spell of their wild nightly cry, long and mournful, coming just as the darkness has fully come, lasting but a few seconds, and then heard no more 'til the night gives place to the fresh sheet of dawn. I have pored in the morning over the big round foot-prints of a mountain lion where he had sneaked in hours of darkness, past my saddle pillowed head. I have hunted much, and killed a little, the wary, the beautiful, the fleet-footed big game. I have driven a four-in-hand over corduroy roads and ridden horseback over the pathless vast wilds of the continent's backbone.

I have been nearly frozen 11,000 feet in air in blinding snow, I have baked on the Dakota plains with the thermome-ter at 116 degrees, and I have met characters as diverse as the climate. I know what it means to be a miner and a cowboy, and have risked my life when need be, but, best of all, I have felt the charm of the glorious freedom, the quick rushing blood, the bounding motion, of the wild life, the joy of the living and of the doing, of the mountain and the plain; I have learned to know and feel some, at least, of the secrets of the Wild Ones. In short, though I am still a woman and may be tender, I am a Woman Tenderfoot no longer.

GRACE GALLATIN SETON

Illustrator N. C. Wyeth's depiction of Stewart and daughter Jerrine as they set out on one of their camping trips, from Letters of a Woman Homesteader.

6

THE WOMAN HOMESTEADER
Elinore Pruitt Stewart
(1876–1933)

*I wanted to just knock about foot-loose
and free to see life as a gypsy sees it. I had
planned to see the Cliff-Dwellers' home;
to live right there until I caught the spirit
of the surroundings enough to live over
their lives in imagination anyway. I had
planned to see the old missions and to go
to Alaska; to hunt in Canada. I even
dreamed of Honolulu. Life stretched out
before me one long, happy jaunt. I aimed
to see all the world I could, but to travel
unknown bypaths to do it.*

 When Elinore Pruitt Rupert and her young daughter, Jerrine, boarded the train to Colorado to see the Cliff Dwellers' homes in Mesa Verde, Rupert intended to write about the newly created national park for the *Kansas City Star*, but her plan went off track immediately. She came down with a virulent fever, and by the time she recovered she was out of money. The divorced single mother headed to Denver to find work. The only jobs available were low-paying domestic positions. She took them, but the allure of adventure stayed with her, tugging her to a world beyond that of her daily existence.

Elinore Pruitt was born in 1876 in the Chickasaw Nation in Indian Territory. Tribal enrollment records suggest that her grandmother, Mary Ann Courtney, was half Chickasaw. Elinore may have briefly attended the only school in that part of the country, but then she taught herself. Elinore's family was poor; she did not own a pair of shoes until she was six.

Elinore was seventeen when her mother died; her stepfather died a year later. Elinore wanted to keep the family together, so she and five unmarried siblings went to live with their grandmother Mary Ann, who also lived in the Chickasaw Nation. "Well, we had no money to hire men to do our work, so [we] had to learn to do it ourselves. Consequently I learned to do many things which girls more fortunately situated don't even know have to be done." As the oldest by several years, Elinore would have taken on the brunt of the hard work. Her hands became "hard, rough, and stained with machine oil" as she learned to run the mowing machine. There was no room for personal vanity, either then or later in her life.

Pruitt worked as a washerwoman for the railroad, and sometime around 1902 she married Harry Rupert, a civil engineer. They filed for land and homesteaded in Indian Territory. Records from that time are incomplete, but it appears that Elinore and Harry were divorced in 1905. In 1906 she was living in Oklahoma City and doing domestic work. Divorce was not something one wanted to make public, so Elinore said her husband had been killed in a railroad accident. She gave birth to Mary Jerrine in February of that year.

Elinore and Jerrine took off for Mesa Verde later in 1906 but instead landed in Denver. Elinore was virtually destitute. She accepted the jobs she could find, usually cleaning, cooking, and performing other housekeeping duties. Like single mothers today, she had the double burden of earning a living and raising her daughter by herself.

She eventually secured a stable position with a retired schoolteacher, Juliet Coney, who later became her confidante. But Elinore remained restless, and after a bout with the "grippe" she realized that she wanted no more of "the rattle and bang, of the glare and the soot, the smells and the hurry" of Denver and that "nothing but the mountains, the pines, and the clean, fresh air seemed worthwhile." She decided to leave Denver and homestead. The idea may have seemed absurd to others, but Elinore had homesteaded before and was prepared to work hard. She did not consider her gender an obstacle.

A friend recommended that she first work as a housekeeper for a rancher to get advice about land and water rights. Elinore answered an ad placed by Clyde Stewart, a Scottish widower who ranched in Burntfork, in southwest Wyoming. Mutual inspection proved favorable, and she and Jerrine accompanied Stewart to the ranch in March 1909. On April 23 Elinore filed on 147 acres adjacent to her employer's ranch, paying $15.51 in fees.

Elinore sent letters to Mrs. Coney, her elderly, housebound friend, describing her new surroundings, life on the ranch, and the trip to Green River to file her claim. Struck by the beauty of the land, her spirit rose in joy. Of the trip to Green River she wrote:

> It was too beautiful a night to sleep, so I put my head out to look and to think. I saw the moon come up and hang for a while over the mountain as if it were discouraged with the prospect, and the big white stars flirted shamelessly with the hills. I saw a coyote come trotting along and felt sorry for him, having to hunt food in so barren a place, but when presently I heard the whirr of wings I felt sorry for the sage chickens he had disturbed. At length a cloud came up and I went to sleep, and next morning was covered with several inches of snow. It didn't hurt us a bit.

For someone who had received little formal education, Elinore worked magic with words. She captured what her senses experienced and created images for her readers, who through her prose could vicariously listen to the coyote and sage chickens, drink in the moon, and wake under a blanket of powdery snow.

Two months after she arrived in Wyoming and less than two weeks after she filed for her land, Elinore married Clyde Stewart. "I had not thought I should ever marry again," she wrote Mrs. Coney in December. "The engagement was powerfully short because both agreed that the trend of events and the ranch work seemed to require that we be married first and do our 'sparking' afterward. You see, we had to chink in the wedding between times, that is, between planting the oats and other work that must be done early or not at all."

Elinore assured Mrs. Coney that the marriage did not mean the end of her homesteading. "I should not have married if Clyde had not promised I should meet all my [proving up] difficulties unaided. I wanted the fun and the experience. For that reason I want to earn every cent that goes into my own land and improvements myself. Sometimes I almost have a brain-storm wondering how I am going to do it, but I know I shall succeed; other women have succeeded."

Elinore's experience with machinery came in handy immediately. Their first summer together her husband panicked because he could not hire anyone to help with the mowing. One morning when he was away Elinore hooked up the horses and "had enough cut before he got back to show him I knew how." Clyde was pleased and gave her the ultimate compliment: Elinore, he said, had "almost as much sense as a 'mon,' and that is an honor I never aspired to, even in my wildest dreams."

The yearning to visit Mesa Verde, California, Canada, and Hawaii faded in the face of the endless rounds of ranch work that claimed Elinore's attention, but her penchant for travel did not abate. If she could not seek adventure in exotic places, she would find it nearby. One September day, after the hay had been put up, she and Jerrine took off into their vast Wyoming backyard:

We got away by sunup and a glorious day we had. We followed a stream higher up into the mountains and the air was so keen and clear at first we had on our coats. There was a tang of sage and of pine in the air, and our horse was midside deep in rabbit-brush, a shrub just covered with flowers that look and smell like goldenrod. The blue distance promised many alluring adventures, so we went along singing and simply gulping in summer.

Stewart continued to find opportunities to explore the mountains of Wyoming, but her jaunts were soon curtailed. She was pregnant and gave birth in February 1910. Little James died, as did a premature daughter later that year; Elinore's grandmother Mary Ann also passed away. But better times followed, as three healthy boys were born in quick succession in 1911, 1912, and 1913.

Stewart kept up a steady stream of letters to Mrs. Coney, who shared them with a friend who was the editor of *Atlantic Monthly*. Ellery Sedgwick had been looking for articles about "interesting happenings by an interesting person" and thought the letters would be a good vehicle, as they were direct and informal. "A Homesteader's Holiday," "A Wedding and Other Matters," "The Story of Cora Belle," "The Adventure of the Christmas Tree," "Horse Thieves," "Calling on the Mormons," and other stories ran in *Atlantic Monthly* from October 1913 through April 1914.

"A Charming Adventure" (following) is from one of Stewart's early letters, written the September after she arrived on the ranch. She was four months pregnant, and Jerrine was three and a half years old at the time. Elinore signed her name Rupert because she had not told her former employer of her marriage to Clyde Stewart.

Elinore's letters struck a cord, not only with Sedgwick but with readers across the country. Elinore's audience loved her unpretentious, engaging descriptions of her home, family, and surroundings. Although one reviewer wrote, "There is no assumption of finished style, no attempt at fine language, no unified plot development, simply the natural recital of incident to the friend [in Denver]," Elinore's letters did not simply fly from her pen. She thought carefully about her readers and what she wanted to say to them. She eschewed fine language because using it would have been inappropriate for her audience and her message. She organized the letters in a unified plot—about her life as a woman homesteader.

It is not clear exactly when Stewart shifted from writing as herself to writing as the Woman Homesteader. At first she intended only to inform and amuse her friend with news from the homestead. But Stewart began substituting fictional names for real ones and developing fictional characters based on people she knew. Eventually, she began dressing up some of her stories, and in later years she wrote "story letters" that contained elements of fiction as well as fact.

By adopting the persona of the Woman Homesteader, Stewart found a way to validate and endorse homesteading as a way of life for single women:

> To me, homesteading is the solution of all poverty's problems, but I realize that temperament has much to do with success in any undertaking, and persons afraid of coyotes and work and loneliness had better let ranching alone. At the same time, any woman who can stand her own company, can see the beauty of the sunset, loves growing things, and is willing to put in as much time at careful labor as she does over the washtub, will certainly succeed; will have independence, plenty to eat all the time, and a home of her own in the end.

In 1914, when Stewart's articles were bundled into a book, *Letters of a Woman Homesteader*, Houghton Mifflin sent her $500—a huge amount of money for a homesteader. Most of the funds went to the ranch, but Stewart kept enough to buy herself a gas lantern. She could only write at night when the ranch and family chores were finished, and a lantern would make that considerably easier. (From this distance it is difficult to appreciate fully the constraints under which Stewart worked. In one letter to a friend, she excused her tardy reply by saying she had run out of paper.)

Stewart's first book was a smashing success. "A readable little book, full of the tang of the prairies and of a delightful personality," wrote the *New York Times*. "Spontaneity is the keynote of all the narration," chimed in the *Nation*. "Good to read aloud to the whole family," said *Dial*. "To a world living in the shadow of carnage and suffering it offers a message the sunny simplicity and kindly good sense of which are delightfully bracing," wrote the *London Athenaeum*. (Years later *A Woman Homesteader* became the basis for the acclaimed movie *Heartland*, and the book continues to please readers to this day.)

Atlantic Monthly commissioned another set of letters, and Elinore wrote about an elk hunt that the Stewarts went on with friends in 1915. Elinore, who was the only woman, focused her attention less on the hunt and more on the country through which she traveled:

> Dawn in the mountains—how I wish I could describe it to you! If I could only make you feel the keen, bracing air, the exhilarating climb; if I could only paint its beauties, what a picture you should have! Here the colors are very different from those of the desert. I suppose the forest makes it so. The shadows are mellow, like the colors in an old picture—greenish amber light and a blue-gray sky. Far ahead of us we could see the red rim of rock of a mountain above the timber line. The first rays of the sun turned the jagged peaks into golden points of a crown.

The letters were also published as a book, *Letters on an Elk Hunt*, in 1915. At this time Elinore also wrote a series of children's stories for *Youth's Companion*.

Stewart could not have known it, but she had reached the pinnacle of her writing career. Perhaps when she turned to writing professionally instead of to a friend she lost the spontaneity that had made her letters so cherished. Perhaps her readers had changed over time and Elinore's sentimentality no longer appealed to them. Whatever the reason, her editor accepted only two more letters for publication, one in 1919 and the other in 1923.

Stewart tried her hand at fiction, finishing a novel, *Sand and Sage*, in 1921. Not surprisingly, the story was set in the ranch land of Wyoming. A mix-up in her address, though, caused her to fail to meet a publisher's offer by the required date. Stewart was devastated. She had lost two valuable opportunities—first, to reach out to her audience, and second, to revive her flagging career.

Whether she published or not, Stewart was still a wife, mother, homesteader, writer, and lover of adventure. In 1916 she took Jerrine— and sometimes her whole family—on camping trips to the mountains near Burntfork. The trips were full of fun and adventure.

Stewart continued writing "story letters," based in reality with some embellishment, to entertain her correspondents and to fulfill her need to write about the images that crowded her brain. Stewart's biographer, Suzanne George, believes the letters show a change in 1919 as Elinore put forth stronger women characters who were more independent and less sentimental. Certainly, Stewart provided a model for other women, regardless of whether they homesteaded.

Between 1917 and 1933 Stewart was busy tending her war garden, selling war bonds, doctoring neighbors, seeing that her children received the best education possible on limited means, taking care of the ranch, and reaching out to those who were less fortunate during the Depression and Dust Bowl era. She could never turn anyone away. "I just love people, I just love to love them," she wrote. But 1930 and 1931 proved challenging, as Jerrine, Clyde, and then Elinore contracted major illnesses.

When Stewart was asked to contribute a piece to a book on folklore in 1932, she decided to put more effort into her writing. Her health no longer allowed her to set off by herself, but her family settled her in a tent in the mountains so she could be reunited with the land that gave her so much joy and offered so much inspiration. Almost immediately she fell ill. Stewart underwent surgery that initially appeared successful, but she died shortly thereafter on October 8, 1933, of a blood clot in her brain.

Stewart never made it to the far-off places of which she had first dreamed, but she found adventure aplenty on a homestead in Wyoming. She pitched into whatever the ranch demanded, whether it was a woman's job or not, and on those rare days when she could take off she renewed her body and soul in her beloved mountains. Elinore Pruitt Stewart treated life itself as an adventure. Whether headed for Mesa Verde—"I wanted to just knock about foot-loose and free to see life as a gypsy sees it"—or for the mountains—"We didn't know where we were going, but we were on our way"—Elinore brimmed with a zest for life.

A Charming Adventure

September 28, 1909

Dear Mrs. Coney,

Your second card just reached me and I am plumb glad because, although I answered your other, I was wishing I could write you, for I have had the most charming adventure.

It is the custom here for as many women as care to to go in a party over into Utah to Ashland (which is over a hundred miles away) after fruit. They usually go in September, and it takes a week to make the trip. They take wagons and camp out and of course have a good time, but, the greater part of the way, there isn't even the semblance of a road and it is merely a semblance anywhere. They came over to invite me to join them. I was of two minds—I wanted to go, but it seemed a little risky and a big chance for discomfort, since we would have to cross the Uinta Mountains, and a snowstorm [would be] likely any time. But I didn't like to refuse outright, so we left it to Mr. Stewart. His "Ye're nae gang" sounded powerful final, so the ladies departed in awed silence and I assumed a martyrlike air and acted like a very much abused woman, although he did only what I wanted him to do. At last, in sheer desperation he told me the "bairn canna stand the treep," and that was why he was so determined. I knew why, of course, but I continued to look abused lest he gets it into his head that he can boss me. After he had been reduced to the proper plane of humility and had explained and begged my pardon and had told me to consult only my own pleasure about going and coming and using his horses, only not to "expoose" the bairn, why, I forgave him and we were friends once more.

Next day all the men left for the roundup, to be gone a week. I knew I never could stand myself a whole week. In a little while the ladies came past on their way to Ashland. They were all laughing and were so happy that I really began to wish I was one of their number, but they went their way and I kept wanting to go *somewhere*. I got reckless and determined to do something real bad. So I went down to the barn and saddled Robin Adair, placed a pack on "Jeems McGregor," then Jerrine and I left for a camping-out expedition.

It was nine o'clock when we started and we rode hard until about four, when I turned Robin loose, saddle and all, for I knew he would go home and someone would see him and put him into the pasture. We had gotten to where we couldn't ride anyway, so I put Jerrine on the pack and led "Jeems" for about two hours longer; then, as I had come to a good place to camp, we stopped.

While we had at least two good hours of daylight, it gets so cold here in the evening that fire is very necessary. We had been climbing higher into the mountains all day and had reached a level tableland where the grass was luxuriant and there was plenty of wood and water. I unpacked "Jeems" and staked him out, built a roaring fire, and made our bed in an angle of a sheer wall of rock where we would be protected against the wind. Then I put some potatoes into the embers, as Baby and I are both fond of roasted potatoes. I started to a little spring to get water for my coffee when I saw a couple of jackrabbits playing, so I went back for my little shotgun. I shot one of the rabbits, so I felt very like Leather-stocking because I had killed but one when I might have gotten two. It was fat and young, and it was but the work of a moment to dress it and hang it up on a tree. Then I fried some slices of bacon, made myself a cup of coffee, and Jerrine and I sat on the ground and ate. Everything smelled and tasted so good! This air is so tonic that one gets delightfully hungry. Afterward we watered and restaked "Jeems," I rolled some logs onto the fire, and then we sat and enjoyed the prospect.

The moon was so new that its light was very dim, but the stars were bright. Presently a long, quivering wail arose and was answered from a dozen hills. It seemed just the sound one ought to hear in such a place. When the howls ceased for a moment we could hear the subdued roar of the creek and the crooning of the wind in the pines. So we rather enjoyed the coyote chorus and were not afraid, because they don't attack people. Presently we crept under our Navajos and, being tired, were soon asleep.

I was awakened by a pebble striking my cheek. Something prowling on the bluff above us had dislodged it and it struck me. By my Waterbury it was four o'clock, so I arose and spitted my rabbit. The logs had left a big bed of coals, but some ends were still burning and had burned in such a manner that the heat would go both under and over my rabbit. So I put plenty of bacon grease over him and hung him up to roast. Then I went back to bed. I didn't want to start early because the air is too keen for comfort early in the morning.

The sun was just gliding the hilltops when we arose. Everything, even the barrenness, was beautiful. We have had frosts, and the quaking aspens were a trembling field of gold as far up the stream as we could see. We were 'way up above them and could look far across the valley. We could see the silvery gold of the willows, the russet and bronze of the currants, the patches of cheerful green showed where the pines were. The splendor was relieved by a background of sober gray-green hills, but even on them gay streaks and patches of yellow showed where rabbit-brush grew. We washed our faces at the spring—the grasses that grew around the edge and dipped into the water were loaded with ice—our rabbit was done to a turn, so I made some delicious coffee, Jerrine got herself a can of water, and we breakfasted. Shortly afterward we started again. We didn't know where we were going, but we were on our way.

That day was more toilsome than the last, but a very happy one. The meadowlarks kept singing like they were glad to see us. But we were still climbing and soon got beyond the larks and sage chickens and up into the timber, where there are lots of grouse. We stopped to noon by a little lake, where I got two small squirrels and a string of trout. We had some trout for dinner and salted the rest with the squirrels in an empty can for future use. I was anxious to get a grouse and kept close watch, but was never quick enough. Our progress was now slower and more difficult, because in places we could scarcely get through the forest. Fallen trees were everywhere and we had to avoid the branches, which was powerful hard to do. Besides, it was quite dusky among the trees long before night, but it was all so grand and awe-inspiring. Occasionally there was an opening through which we could see the snowy peaks, seemingly just beyond us, toward which we were headed. But when you get among such grandeur you get to feel how little you are and how foolish is human endeavor, except that which reunites us with the mighty force called God. I was plumb uncomfortable, because all my own efforts have always been just to make the best of everything and to take things as they come.

At last we came to an open side of the mountain where the trees were scattered. We were facing south and east, and the mountain we were on sheered away in a dangerous slant. Beyond us still greater wooded mountains blocked the way, and in the cañon between night had already fallen. I began to get scary. I could only think of bears and catamounts, so, as it was five o'clock, we decided to camp. The trees were immense. The lower branches came clear to the ground and grew so dense that any tree afforded a splendid shelter from the weather, but I was nervous and wanted one that would protect us against any possible attack. At last we found one growing in a crevice of what seemed to be a sheer wall of rock. Nothing could reach us on two sides, and in front two large trees had fallen so that I could make a log heap which would give us warmth and make us safe. So with rising spirits I unpacked and prepared for the night. I soon had a roaring fire up against the logs and, cutting away a few branches, let the heat into as snug a bedroom as anyone could wish. The pine needles made as soft a carpet as the wealthiest could afford. Springs abound in the mountains, so water was plenty. I staked "Jeems" quite near so that the firelight would frighten away any wild thing that tried to harm him. Grass was very plentiful, so when he was made "comfy" I made our bed and fried our trout. The branches had torn off the bag in which I had my bread, so it was lost in the forest, but who needs bread when they have good, mealy potatoes? In a short time we were eating like Lent was just over. We lost all the glory of the sunset except what we got by reflection, being on the side of the mountain as we were, with the dense woods

ELINORE PRUITT STEWART

between. Big sullen clouds kept drifting over and a wind got lost in the trees that kept them rocking and groaning in a horrid way. But we were just as cozy as we could be and rest was as good as anything.

I wish you could once sleep on the kind of bed we enjoyed that night. It was both soft and firm, with the clean, spicy smell of the pine. The heat from our big fire came in and we were warm as toast. It was so good to stretch out and rest. I kept thinking how superior I was since I dared to take such an outing when so many poor women down in Denver were bent on making their twenty cents per hour in order that they could spare a quarter to go to the "show." I went to sleep with a powerfully self-satisfied feeling, but I awoke to realize that pride goeth before a fall.

I could hardly remember where I was when I awoke, and I could almost hear the silence. Not a tree moaned, not a branch seemed to stir. I arose and my head came in violent contact with a snag that was not there when I went to bed. I thought either I must have grown tall or the tree shorter during the night. As soon as I peered out, the mystery was explained.

Such a snowstorm I never saw! The snow had pressed the branches down lower, hence my bumped head. Our fire was burning merrily and the heat kept the snow from in front. I scrambled out and poked up the fire; then, as it was only five o'clock, I went back to bed. And then I began to think how many kinds of idiot I was. Here I was 30 or 40 miles from home, in the mountains where no one goes in the winter and where I knew the snow got to be 10 or 15 feet deep. But I could never see the good of moping, so I got up and got breakfast while Baby put her shoes on. We had our squirrels and more baked potatoes and I had delicious black coffee.

After I had eaten I felt more hopeful. I knew Mr. Stewart would hunt for me if he knew I was lost. It was true, he wouldn't know which way to start, but I determined to rig up "Jeems" and turn him loose, for I knew he would go home and that he would leave a trail so that I could be found. I hated to do so, for I knew I should always have to be powerfully humble afterward. Anyway it was still snowing, great, heavy flakes; they looked as large as dollars. I didn't want to start "Jeems" until the snow stopped because I wanted him to leave a clear trail. I had sixteen loads for my gun and I reasoned that I could likely kill enough food to last twice that many days by being careful what I shot at. It just kept snowing, so at last I decided to take a little hunt and provide for the day. I left Jerrine happy with the towel rolled into a baby, and went along the brow of the mountain for almost a mile, but the snow fell so thickly that I couldn't see far. Then I happened to look down into the cañon that lay east of us and saw smoke. I looked toward it a long time, but could make out nothing but smoke, but presently I heard a dog bark and I knew I was near a camp of some kind. I resolved to join them, so went back to break my own camp.

At last everything was ready and Jerrine and I both mounted. Of all the times! If you think there is much comfort, or even security, in riding a packhorse in a snowstorm over mountains where there is no road, you are plumb wrong. Every once in a while a tree would unload its snow down our backs. "Jeems" kept stumbling and threatening to break our necks. At last we got down the mountainside, where new danger confronted us—we might lose sight of the smoke or ride into a bog. But at last, after what seemed hours, we came into a "clearing" with a small log house and, what is rare in Wyoming, a fireplace. Three or four hounds set up their deep baying, and I knew by the chimney and the

ELINORE PRUITT STEWART

hounds that it was the home of a southerner. A little old man came bustling out, chewing his tobacco so fast, and almost frantic about his suspenders, which it seemed he couldn't get adjusted.

As I rode up, he said, "Whither, friend?" I said "Hither." Then he asked, "Air you spying around for one of them dinged game wardens arter that deer I killed yisteddy?" I told him I had never even seen a game warden and that I didn't know he had killed a deer. "Wall," he said, "air you spying around arter that gold mine I diskivered over on the west side of Baldy?" But after a while I convinced him that I was no more nor no less than a foolish woman lost in the snow. Then he said, "Light, stranger, and look at your saddle." So I "lit" and looked, and then I asked him what part of the South he was from. He answered, "Yell County, by gum! The best place in the United States, or in the world, either." That was my introduction to Zebulon Pike Parker.

Only two "Johnny Rebs" could have enjoyed each other's company as Zebulon Pike and myself did. He was so small and so old, but so cheerful and so sprightly, and a real southerner! He had a big, open fireplace with backlogs and andirons. How I enjoyed it all! How we feasted on some of the deer killed "yisteddy," and real corn pone baked in a skillet down on the hearth. He was so full of happy recollections and had a few that were not so happy! He is, in some way, a kinsman of Pike of Pike's Peak fame, and he came west "jist arter the wah" on some expedition and "jist stayed." He told me about his home life back in Yell County, and I feel that I know all the "young uns." . . .

At last it came out that he had not heard from home since he left it. "Don't you ever write?" I asked. "No, I am not an eddicated man, although I started to school. Yes'm, I started along of the rest, but they told me it was a Yankee teacher and I was 'fraid, so when I got most to the school-house I hid in the bushes with my spelling book, so that is all the learning I ever got. But my mother was an eddicated woman, yes'm, she could both read and write. I have the Bible she give me yit. Yes'm, you jist wait and I'll show you." After some rummaging in a box he came back with a small leather-bound Bible with print so small it was hard to read. After turning to the record of births and deaths he handed it to me, his wrinkled old face shining with pride as he said, "There, my mother wrote that with her own hand." I took the book and after a little deciphered that "Zebulon Pike Parker was born Feb. 10, 1830," written in the stiff, difficult style of long ago and written with pokeberry ink. He said his mother used to read about some "old feller that was jist covered with biles," so I read Job to him, and he was full of surprise they didn't "get some cherry bark and some sasparilly and bile it good and gin it to him."

He had a side room to his cabin, which was his bed-room; so that night he spread down a buffalo robe and two bearskins before the fire for Jerrine and me. After making sure there were no moths in them, I spread blankets over them and put a sleepy, happy little girl to bed, for he had in-sisted on making molasses candy for her because they hap-pened to be born on the same day of the month. And then he played the fiddle until almost one o'clock. He played all the simple, sweet, old-time pieces, in rather a squeaky, jerky way, I am afraid, but the music suited the time and the place.

Next morning he called me early and when I went out I saw such a beautiful sunrise, well worth the effort of coming to see. I had thought his cabin in a cañon, but the snow had deceived me, for a few steps from the door the mountains seemed to drop down suddenly for several hundred feet and the first of the snow peaks seemed to lie right at our feet.

Around its base is a great swamp, in which the swamp pines grow very thickly and from which a vapor was rising that got about halfway up the snow peak all around. Fancy to yourself a big jewel box of dark green velvet lined with silver chiffon, the snow peak lying like an immense opal in its center and over all the amber light of a new day. That is what it looked most like.

Well, we next went to the corral, where I was surprised to find about thirty head of sheep. Some of them looked like they should have been sold ten years before. "Don't you ever sell any of your sheep?" I asked. "No'm. There was a feller come here once and wanted to buy some of my wethers, but I wouldn't sell any because I didn't need any money." Then he went from animal to animal, caressing each and talking to them, calling them each by name. He milked his one cow, fed his two little mules, and then we went back to the house to cook breakfast. We had delicious venison steak, smoking hot, and hoecakes and the "bestest" coffee, and honey.

After breakfast we set out for home. Our pack transferred to one of the little mules, we rode "Jeems," and Mr. Parker rode the other mule. He took us another way, down cañon after cañon, so that we were able to ride all the time and could make better speed. We came down out of the snow and camped within 12 miles of home in an old, deserted ranch house. We had grouse and sage chicken for supper. I was so anxious to get home that I could hardly sleep, but at last I did and was only awakened by the odor of coffee, and barely had time to wash before Zebulon Pike called breakfast. Afterward we fixed "Jeems's" pack so that I could still ride, for Zebulon Pike was very anxious to get back to his "critters."

Poor, lonely, childlike little man! He tried to tell me how glad he had been to entertain me. "Why," he said, "I was plumb glad to see you and right sorry to have you go." . . .

I got home at twelve and found, to my joy, that none of the men had returned, so I am safe from their superiority for a while, at least.

With many apologies for this outrageous letter, I am

Your ex-Washlady,

Elinore Rupert

Mary Roberts Rinehart in 1915, from her book Through Glacier Park.

7

ADVENTURES OF AN AUTHOR
Mary Roberts Rinehart

(1876–1958)

If you are normal and philosophical; if
you love your country; if you like bacon,
or will eat it anyhow; if you are willing
to learn how little you count in the
eternal scheme of things; if you are
prepared, for the first day or two, to be
able to locate every muscle in your body
and a few extra ones that seem to have
crept in and are crowding, go ride in the
Rocky Mountains and save your soul.

Mary Roberts Rinehart's first trip to Glacier National Park in 1915 left a vivid, lasting imprint. She entered the wilderness as a reporter, there to chronicle the first expedition into the newly established park. The trip was not easy. Rinehart traveled 300 miles on horseback through some of the most rugged terrain in the Rocky Mountains. Having just returned from horrific scenes on the front lines of World War I—where she was the first correspondent, male or female, to report from the line of battle—Rinehart viewed the Glacier Park expedition as an antidote to the images that haunted her and a chance to escape the demands of the world.

From her youngest years Rinehart had been given liberties that others looked upon with disapproving eyes. Her progressive parents, Cornelia (Gilleland) Roberts and Tom Roberts, bought her a "safety" bicycle—the second girl's bike in Philadelphia. Neighbors were scandalized, exclaiming that for a girl bicycling was "improper and immodest" and would make Mary "bold." Cornelia, in turn, made Mary a bicycling costume and allowed her to explore new neighborhoods. Such freedom was unheard of for a young girl in the late nineteenth century, and it opened Mary's mind to the world around her; it also expanded her dreams. Her thoughts were "a queer jumble of romance, adventure and already a driving ambition to 'do something' . . . to travel and adventure, to shoot and ride, to explore far places."

As she grew older Mary thought about becoming a writer or a doctor, but her plans were thwarted by the family's gradual slide into genteel poverty after her father lost his job. Knowing that a writing career was risky and impractical—and without money for an expensive medical education—Mary had few options. Women at her social level were financially helpless. They might do needlework, accept boarders, or teach, but they did not become clerks or factory workers. They were expected to marry and be supported by their husbands. Mary chose instead to become a nurse, despite her mother's protests that nursing was an unsuitable occupation for women with Mary's respectable background. During her training Mary met Stanley Rinehart, a surgeon. Three years later, after she graduated, the two were married.

Her husband ran his private practice in their home. The couple soon had three sons as well. Family life left scant time for anything else, and Rinehart felt increasingly like "the household drudge I was." She

Rinehart's party crossing Triple Divide, from her book Through Glacier National Park.

revisited her earlier thoughts of writing and penned several poems that were subsequently published. Then she turned to fiction, spinning out mystery stories in magazines—all the while demurring that she was not out to develop a career but only wanted to earn extra money for the family. A publisher accepted the manuscript of her first book; she continued to write, she gained a following, and her books began appearing on the best-seller list. Freedom of character, spirit, intellect, and gender infused many of her stories, particularly those of the beloved character Letitia "Tish" Carberry who delighted readers of the *Saturday Evening Post* for nearly thirty years.

Tish was Mary's alter ego, a woman who did everything that Mary might have done had she not married. When Rinehart was in Glacier Park she was forced by custom to wear an awkward riding suit with a divided skirt. When she dismounted she hid behind her horse and buttoned up the skirt so as not to transgress the rules of decorum. Tish, on the other hand, says outright: "I've felt for a long time that I'd be glad to discard skirts. Skirts are badges of servitude, survivals of the harem, reminders of a time when nothing was expected of women but parasitic leisure." Moreover, Tish does what Mary could not do and abandons the divided skirt for riding:

> "I'm so glad wide skirts have come in," said [Mrs. Ostermaier, the minister's wife]. "They're so modest, aren't they, Miss Tish?"
>
> "Not in a wind," Tish said, eyeing her coldly.
>
> "I do think, dear Miss Tish," she went on with her eyes down, "that to—to go about in riding-breeches before a young man is—well, it is hardly discrete, is it?"
>
> "If it was any treat to a twenty-four-year-old cowpuncher to see three elderly women in riding-breeches, Mrs. Ostermaier—and it's kind of you to think so—why, I'm not selfish."

Tish has scored her point, the reader has chuckled, and Rinehart has pushed gently at the conventions that bound women in her day.

But some conventions proved more challenging. Rinehart enjoyed writing immensely, but it posed a moral conundrum she could not discuss with anyone because she could not acknowledge it to herself. She insisted that she was devoted to her family—family always came first. She was "no feminist" and had no use for "those women who would throw everything overboard for the career; no pity for their ill-balanced lives, no sympathy for their achievement." Yet increasingly Rinehart's work took her away from home for days, even weeks at a time. Ambition usually overrode her guilt, but whenever she faced the public she portrayed herself as a wife and mother first and a writer second. She managed to juggle family and career but had to do "four times as much as any woman I know." She was essentially the supermom of her day.

When Rinehart returned from Glacier Park exclaiming that the trip had renewed her, she naturally wanted to go back. In a move that may have eased her guilt, she took Stan and the three children with her so she could be a wife, mother, and writer all at once. In 1916 Rinehart and her family joined Howard Eaton in Glacier Park for a two-week shakedown trip during which the boys learned to ride and became familiar with trail life. The Rineharts then split off on their own adventure, for they had an ambitious plan to ride through the western part of the park and run a section of the North Fork of the Flathead River, then travel to Washington State and cross the Cascades on horseback.

Rinehart's accounts of her travels (see "Running the Flathead Rapids" and "Lyman Lake and Cloudy Pass" from *Tenting Tonight: A Chronicle of Sport and Adventure in Glacier Park and the Cascade Mountains*, following) are markedly different from those of the other women presented in this book. Whereas Dora Keen minimizes the difficulties of climbing a 16,000-foot mountain, Rinehart plays to her audience—to those readers who think, for instance, that running the "riotous, debauched, and highly erratic" Flathead River is absurd. Rinehart downplays the fact that she has arranged for this adventure; she writes that she proceeds with trepidation, only at the insistence of her family. Later, while climbing to Cloudy Pass, she can barely make it: "I confided to [Stan], between gasps, that I was dying," she tells readers.

Yet Rinehart gives herself away when she contemplates the arrival of Mr. and Mrs. Fred, who joined the Rineharts for the Cascades leg of the trip. "I was accustomed to roughing it; but how about another woman? Would she be putting up her hair in curlers every night, and whimpering when, as sometimes happens, the slow gait of her horse became intolerable?" Rinehart may whimper to her readers, but she draws the line at traveling companions who whimper to her.

For years to come expeditions to the backcountry provided Rinehart with respite from everyday demands, gave her material for books and novels, and fed her appetite for adventure. She fished for salmon in Puget Sound, canoed in Canada, ventured after mountain sheep in Mexico, caught tarpon in Central America, rode horseback in the mountains of Costa Rica, and visited Eaton's dude ranch in Wyoming.

Rinehart had become a famous writer, playwright, and journalist. Publishers offered her plum assignments and paid her well for them. In 1917 she earned close to $100,000—an astonishing sum for anyone at that time, let alone a woman—and her earnings continued to climb.

But by the mid-1920s Rinehart faced a crisis. The secure center of her world—her family—was breaking apart. Her sons had grown up and left home. Her mother had died in a tragic accident. Her husband was no longer even the nominal provider for the family, as he had given up medicine to become her manager. Rinehart was approaching menopause and "old age." (Tish Carberry, after all, was fifty, and she was an "old lady." Mary, at forty-five, was not far behind.) Rinehart also struggled with the fact that her serious fiction had not met with the success her lighter mystery novels had achieved.

Rinehart experienced a serious bout of depression and virtually stopped writing. It was not until Stan signed them up for a camel caravan across Egypt that her spirits rose. She returned refreshed, with abundant new material to inspire her writing.

By 1931 Stan's health was beginning to fail, and he died a year later. In a letter declining Grace Gallatin Seton's invitation to attend an international women writers' conclave, Rinehart wrote that she found it hard to continue alone and was "hoping to spend the summer in some remote spot where I can find both health and peace."

A radical mastectomy in 1936 led Rinehart to broach the forbidden subject of breast cancer in an interview "I Had Cancer," which ran in *Ladies' Home Journal*. The interview brought a far greater public response than any of her books or articles, "So perhaps I have done some good, as I had hoped."

Rinehart continued writing into the mid-1950s to the extent her deteriorating health allowed. In 1954 the Mystery Writers of America gave her a special tribute for her work. She died in her sleep four years later on September 22, 1958, in New York.

Mary Roberts Rinehart wrote over fifty books, twelve of which appeared on the best-seller list; seven plays for stage, radio, and TV; and innumerable articles and editorials. She was a celebrity and one of the highest-paid writers in the United States. Whereas women like Martha Whitman and Pauline Johnson, who also chose careers, forfeited marriage, Rinehart married and slid sideways into a career. She could not frankly recognize her ambition; she wrote, she said, to provide extra money for the grand homes, educational opportunities, and extras her family deserved. In the same way she could not adventure for the sake of adventuring, but she couched trips to the wilderness in terms of fulfilling writing assignments and vacationing with her family. In reality, though, these trips fulfilled her lifelong need "to travel and adventure . . . and explore far places."

Running the Flathead Rapids

We were headed now for the Flathead just south of the Canadian line. To reach the river, it was necessary to take the boats through a burnt forest, without a trail of any sort. They leaped and plunged as the wagon scrambled, jerked, careened, stuck, detoured, and finally got through. There were miles of such going—heartbreaking miles—and at the end we paused at the top of a 60-foot cliff and looked down at the river.

Now, I like water in a tub or drinking glass or under a bridge. I am very keen about it. But I like still water—quiet, well-behaved, stay-at-home water. The North Fork of the Flathead River is a riotous, debauched, and highly erratic stream. It staggers in a series of wild zigzags for a hundred miles of waterway from the Canadian border to Columbia Falls, our destination. And that hundred miles of whirlpools, jagged rocks, and swift and deadly cañons we were to travel. I turned around and looked at the Family. It was my ambition that had brought them to this. We might never again meet, as a whole. We were sure to get to Columbia Falls, but not at all sure to get there in the boats. I looked at the boats; they were, I believe, stout riverboats. But they were small. Undeniably, they were very small.

The river appeared to be going about 90 miles an hour. There was one hope, however. Perhaps they could not get the boats down over the bluff. It seemed a foolhardy thing even to try. I suggested this to Bob. But he replied, rather tartly, that he had not brought those boats at the risk of his life through all those miles of wilderness to have me fail him now.

He painted the joys of the trip. He expressed so strong a belief in them that he said that he himself would ride with the outfit, thus permitting most of the Family in the boats that first day. He said the river was full of trout. I expressed a strong doubt that any trout could live in that stream and hold their own. I felt that they had all been washed down years ago. And again I looked at the Family.

Because I knew what would happen. The Family would insist on going along. It was not going to let mother take this risk alone; it was going to drown with her if necessary.

The Family jaws were set. *They were going.*

The entire outfit lowered the wagon by roping it down. There was one delicious moment when I thought boats and all were going over the edge. But the ropes held. Nothing happened.

They put the boats in the water.

I had one last rather pitiful thought as I took my seat in the stern of one of them.

"This is my birthday," I said wistfully. "It's rather a queer way to spend a birthday, I think."

But this was met with stern silence. I was to have my story whether I wanted it or not.

Yet once in the river, the excitement got me. I had run brief spells of rapids before. There had been a gasp or two and it was over. But this was to be a prolonged four days' gasp, with intervals only to sleep at night.

Fortunately for all of us, it began rather quietly. The current was swift, so that, once out into the stream, we shot ahead as if we had been fired out of a gun. But, for all that, the upper reaches were comparatively free of great rocks. Friendly little sandy shoals beckoned to us. The water was shallow. But, even then, I noticed what afterward I found was to be a delusion of the entire trip.

This was the impression of riding downhill. I do not remember how much the Flathead falls per mile. I have an impression that it is 90 feet, but as that would mean a drop of 9,000 feet, or almost 2 miles, during the trip, I must be wrong somewhere. It was 16 feet, perhaps.

But hour after hour, on the straight stretches, there was that sensation, on looking ahead, of staring down a toboggan slide. It never grew less. And always I had the impression that just beyond that glassy slope the roaring meant uncharted falls—and destruction. It never did.

The outfit, following along the trail, was to meet us at night and have camp ready when we appeared—if we appeared. Only a few of us could use the boats. George Locke [a guide] in one, Mike Shannon [another guide] in the other, could carry two passengers each. For the sake of my story, I was to take the entire trip; the others were to alternate.

I do not know, but I am very confident that no other woman has ever taken this trip. I am fairly confident that no other men have ever taken it. We could find no one who had heard of it being taken. All that we knew was that it was the

MARY ROBERTS RINEHART

North Fork of the Flathead River, and that if we stayed afloat long enough, we would come out at Columbia Falls. The boatmen knew the lower part of the river, but not the upper two-thirds of it.

Now that it is over, I would not give up my memory of that long run for anything. It was one of the most unique experiences in a not uneventful career. It was beautiful always, terrible occasionally. There were dozens of places each day where the boatmen stood up, staring ahead for the channel, while the boats dodged wildly ahead. But always these skillful pilots of ours found a way through. And so fast did we go that the worst places were always behind us before we had time to be really terrified.

The Flathead River in these upper reaches is fairly alive with trout. On the second day, I think it was, I landed a bull-trout that weighed 9 pounds, and got it with a 6-ounce rod. I am very proud of that. I have eleven different pictures of myself holding the fish up. There were trout everywhere. The difficulty was to stop the boat long enough to get them. In fact, we did not stop, save in an occasional eddy in the midst of the torrent. We whipped the stream as we flew along. Under great boulders, where the water seethed and roared, under deep cliffs where it flew like a mill race, there were always fish.

It was frightful work for the boatmen. It required skill every moment. There was not a second in the day when they could relax. Only men trained to river rapids could have done it, and few, even, of these. To the eternal credit of George and Mike, we got through. It was nothing else.

On the evening of the first day, in the dusk which made the river doubly treacherous, we saw our campfire far ahead.

With the going down of the sun, the river had grown cold. We were wet with spray, cramped from sitting still and holding on. But friendly hands drew our boats to shore and helped us out. . . .

On the third day, we went through the Flathead River cañon. We had looked forward to this, both because of its beauty and its danger. Bitterly complaining, the junior members of the family were exiled to the trail with the exception of the Big Boy.

In one of the very greatest stretches of the rapids, a long straightaway, we saw a pygmy figure, far ahead, hailing us from the bank. Behind this pygmy figure stretched a cliff, more than 100 feet in height, of sheer rock overgrown with bushes. The figure had apparently but room on which to stand. George stood up and surveyed the prospect.

"Well," he said, in his slow drawl, "if that's lunch, I don't think we can hit it."

The river was racing at mad speed. Great rocks caught the current, formed whirlpools and eddies, turned us 'round again and again, and sent us spinning on, drenched with spray. That part of the river the boatmen knew—at least by reputation. It had been the scene, a few years before, of the tragic drowning of a man they knew. For now we were getting down into the better-known portions.

To check a boat in such a current seemed impossible. But we needed food. We were tired and cold, and we had a long afternoon's work still before us.

At last, by tremendous effort and great skill, the boatmen made the landing. It was the college boy who had clambered down the cliff and brought the lunch, and it was he who caught the boats as they were whirling by. We had to cling like limpets to the edge, and work our way over to where there was room to sit down.

We made the inevitable cocoa, warmed beans, ate a part of the cheese, and, with gingersnaps and canned fruit, managed to eke out a frugal repast. And shrieked our words over the roar of the river.

It was here that the boats were roped down. Critical examination and long debate with the boatmen showed no way through. On the far side, under the towering cliff, was an opening in the rocks through which the river boiled in a drop of 20 feet.

So it was fortunate, after all, that we had been hailed from the shore and had stopped, dangerous as it had been. For not one of us would have lived had we essayed that passage under the cliff. The Flathead River is not a deep river; the force of its flow is so great, its drop so rapid, that the most powerful swimmer is hopeless in such a current. Light as our flies were, again and again they were swept under and held as though by a powerful hand.

Another year, the Flathead may be a much simpler proposition to negotiate. Owing to the unusually heavy snows of last winter, which had not commenced to melt on the mountaintops until July, the river was high. In a normal summer, I believe that this trip could be taken—though always the boatmen must be expert in river rapids—with comparative safety and enormous pleasure.

There is a thrill and exultation about running rapids— not for minutes, for an hour or two, but for days—that gets into the blood. And when to that exultation is added the most beautiful scenery in America, the trip becomes well worthwhile. However, I am not at all sure that it is a trip for a woman to take. I can swim, but that would not have helped at all had the boat, at any time in those four days, struck a rock and turned over. Nor would the men of the party, all powerful swimmers, have had any more chance than I.

We were a little nervous that afternoon. The cañon

grew wilder; the current, if possible, more rapid. But there were fewer rocks; the riverbed was clearer.

We were rapidly nearing the Middle Fork. Another day would see us there, and from that point, the river, although swift, would lose much of its danger.

Late the afternoon of the third day we saw our camp well ahead, on a ledge above the river. Everything was in order when we arrived. We unloaded ourselves solemnly out of the boats, took our fish, our poles, our graft hooks and landing nets, our fly books, my sunburn lotion, and our weary selves up the bank. Then we solemnly shook hands all around. We had come through; the rest was easy.

Lyman Lake and Cloudy Pass

Now and then there are scenes in the mountains that defy the written word. The view from Cloudy Pass is one; the outlook from Cascade Pass is another. But for sheer loveliness there are few things that surpass Lyman Lake at sunset, its great glacier turned to pink, the towering granite cliffs which surround it dark purple below, bright rose at the summits. And lying there, still with the stillness of the ages, the quiet lake.

Set in its encircling, snow-covered mountains, it lies 5,500 feet above sea level. We had come up in two days from 1,100 feet, a considerable climb. That night, for the first time, we saw the northern lights—at first, one band like a cold finger set across the sky, then others, shooting ribbons of cold fire, now bright, now dim, covering the northern horizon and throwing into silhouette the peaks over our heads. . . .

Rising early is a theory of mine. I approve of it. But I do not consider it rising early to get up at three o'clock in the morning. Three o'clock in the morning is late at night. The moon was still up. It was frightfully cold. My shoes were damp and refused to go on. I could not find any hairpins. And I recalled a number of stories of the extreme disagreeableness of bears when not shot in a vital spot.

With all our hurry, it was four o'clock when we were ready to start. No sun was in sight, but already a faint rose-colored tint was on the tops of the mountains.

We climbed. Then we climbed some more. Then we kept on climbing. Mr. Fred led the way. He had the energy of a high-powered car and the hopefulness of a pacifist. From ledge to ledge he scrambled, turning now and then to wave an encouraging hand. It was not long before I ceased to have strength to wave back. Hours went on. Five hundred feet, 1,000 feet, 1,500 feet above the lake. I confided to the Head [Stan], between gasps, that I was dying. We had seen no living thing; we continued to see no living thing. Two thousand feet, 2,500 feet. There was not enough air in the world to fill my collapsed lungs.

Once Mr. Fred found a track, and scurried off in a new direction. Still no result. The sun was up by that time, and I judged that it was about noon. It was only six-thirty.

A sort of desperation took possession of us all. We would keep up with Mr. Fred or die trying. And then, suddenly, we were on the very roof of the world, on the top of Cloudy Pass. All the kingdoms of the earth lay stretched out around us, and all the kingdoms of the earth were empty.

Now, the usual way to climb Cloudy Pass is to take a good businesslike horse and sit on his back. Then, by devious and circuitous routes, with frequent rests, the horse takes you up. When there is a place the horse cannot manage, you get off and hold its tail, and he pulls you. Even at that, it is a long business and a painful one. But it is better—oh, far, far better!—than the way we had taken.

Have you ever reached a point where you fix your starting eyes on a shrub or a rock 10 feet ahead and struggle for it? And, having achieved it, fix on another 5 feet farther on, and almost fail to get to it? Because, if you have not, you know nothing of this agony of tearing lungs and hammering heart and throbbing muscles that is the mountain climber's price for achievement. . . .

As we sat panting on Cloudy Pass, the sun rose over the cliff of the great granite bowl. The peaks turned from red to yellow. It was absolutely silent. No trees rustled in the morning air. There were no trees. Only, here and there a few stunted evergreens, 2 or 3 feet high, had rooted on the rock and clung there, gnarled and twisted from their winter struggles.

Ears that had grown tired of the noises of cities grew rested. But our ears were more rested than our bodies.

I have always believed that it is easier to go downhill than to go up. This is not true. I say it with the deepest earnestness. After the first 500 feet of descent, progress down became agonizing. The something that had gone wrong with my knees became terribly wrong; they showed a tendency to bend backward; they shook and quivered.

The last mile of that 4-mile descent was one of the most dreadful experiences of my life. A broken thing, I crept into camp and tendered mute apologies to Budweiser, my horse, called familiarly "Buddy." (Although he was not the sort of horse one really became familiar with.)

The remainder of that day, Mrs. Fred and I lay under a mosquito canopy, played solitaire, and rested our aching bodies. . . . The next day we crossed Cloudy Pass and started down the Agnes Creek Valley. It was to be a forced march of 25 miles over a trail which no one was sure existed.

MARY ROBERTS RINEHART

Mary Jobe in the Canadian Rockies.

8

MY QUEST IN THE CANADIAN ROCKIES

Mary Jobe

(1878–1966)

It began at Winnipeg in June. "Why shouldn't we go in and have a look at that big mountain?" Miss Springate and I had asked each other. She, a hardy Englishwoman, was keen for roughing it; I was at home on the trail. It was inevitable that our trip should materialize into something worthwhile. All winter, a trip into the Mount Robson country was uppermost in our minds.

Today's travelers have such easy access to guide-books, maps, computer mapping, and the global positioning system that it is hard to imagine a time when such aids to navigation were not available. Less than 100 years ago, however, great stretches of the globe were labeled "Unmapped Terrain." The native people of each area knew the countryside intimately, but for explorers and their sponsors the only way to obtain a clear idea of the location of mountains, rivers, and other natural features was to go there and find out. On a series of expeditions from 1909 to 1917, Mary Jobe ventured into the wilderness of British Columbia to explore and map sections of the Canadian Rockies, collect botanical information, and study the culture of the Native Americans who lived there.

Mary Jobe was the younger daughter of Sarah (Pittis) Jobe and Richard Jobe. Although "carefully reared," she knew at an early age that she would not be content with the options then available to women. "I had always wanted to be a boy and travel to strange places and do manly things. I hated dolls and petticoats and was happy only with my horses and dogs, roaming through the forests and across the Ohio hills among the Indian graves on my father's farm." She was also fascinated by the land of the Zulu warriors in Africa and wanted to visit there someday.

Jobe was an established academic when she turned to exploration. She had graduated from Scio (later Mount Union), had done graduate work at Bryn Mawr College, and had received a Master of Arts degree from Columbia in English and American history in 1909. Concurrent with her graduate studies she had taught history at several colleges, including Hunter; after graduation she continued to teach at Hunter for seven more years.

The year 1909 marked a change in Jobe's direction. She had once spent three months in British Columbia with college friends in a program led by a botanist from the University of Pennsylvania. That experience introduced her to a new and intriguing land, and when she received an invitation in 1909 to return on an expedition sponsored by the Dominion Topographical Society, she accepted. The expedition's goals were to explore the headwaters of the Gold River and to climb Mount Sir Sandford, in the Selkirk Mountains in British Columbia. The group succeeded in the first goal but failed to reach the summit of

Mount Sir Sandford. At the end of the summer Jobe attended the annual get-together of the Alpine Club of Canada. In 1910 she returned to British Columbia, venturing to the Mount Assiniboine area and then to the Red Deer River; in 1912 she went on a pack trip to Jasper.

These experiences gave Jobe a grounding in wilderness travel and prepared her to explore on her own. In 1913 she undertook an ethnographic expedition to gather material on the customs of Native Americans in northern British Columbia and Alaska. With two Indian guides, she traveled for ten weeks and took copious notes on everything she saw. Jobe's journey into the far reaches of the continent earned her admiration and respect back home.

In 1914 Jobe secured a commission from the Canadian government to explore and map the Fraser watershed in British Columbia. She had a particular interest in climbing a peak she called Mount Kitchie, Cree for "great" or "mighty," later officially named Mount Sir Alexander. Jobe asked her friend Margaret Springate to accompany her. Springate was a rugged Englishwoman who, like Mary, was a member of the Alpine Club of Canada. "Obviously, here was a chance for personal achievement—not merely achievement for public approbation, but achievement for our own pure delight. Here was a chance to see what on the government maps was only a blank white space," Jobe later wrote.

Jobe, Springate, and guides Donald Phillips and Bert Wilkins made up the party. Phillips was a well-known local guide and trapper who had attempted to climb the formidable Mount Robson and had explored on his own. (Several years later Phillips guided Marion Randall Parsons when she climbed in the Robson area.) The four travelers set out on saddle horses, with packhorses to carry the food and equipment; however, "there are many places where the 'passenger' from motives of comfort, precaution, or sheer fright will prefer to walk and lead the cayuse," Jobe noted. "In fact, even in easy mountain travel I infinitely prefer to walk more than half the way." As the party set out from the railroad station near Mount Robson and traveled about 200 miles to the northwest to Mount Kitchie, there were ample opportunities for walking.

Mary Jobe climbing Mount Kitchie, 1914.

The four went as far as they could by horse and then faced the daunting task of bushwhacking onward to the mountain (see "My Quest in the Canadian Rockies," following, which recounts the backpacking section of the trip). Devil's club, which Jobe mentions, is a spine-covered plant that grows thickly in the Northwest and Alaska. The spines pierce clothing, lacerating and breaking off in the skin and causing painful welts. Adverse weather plagued the travelers, and they ran out of food. When an avalanche pitched debris in front of Jobe and Phillips, they realized the terrain was too hazardous for their limited equipment. They had learned much about the region, but Mount Kitchie remained unclimbed.

Jobe's expeditions in 1913 and 1914 contrast sharply with Annie Peck's trips to South America ten years earlier. In 1913 Jobe spent a summer with two Native American guides, apparently without problems and untroubled by what others might think. Peck had needed to take a white male on her expeditions to ensure propriety and to manage the Native American porters. Jobe (like Dora Keen) did not report experiencing prejudice from male colleagues, instead writing of Phillips in glowing terms. Peck, on the other hand, could not command the respect of her Swiss guides. The difference may have resulted in part from the guides themselves. Peck's Swiss imports were steeped in an alpine tradition that considered the mountains to be a man's world. Phillips was from a different generation; he developed his climbing skills in British Columbia and may have been more open to accepting people on their merits rather than their sex.

Jobe returned to Mount Kitchie the next summer but again was unsuccessful in gaining the summit. The Canadian government did, however, name a nearby peak Mount Jobe in her honor. Jobe also became a fellow of the Royal Geographic Society of London.

In the winter of 1917 Jobe joined Phillips and his assistant on a 400-mile winter expedition to the Mount Kitchie area. A newcomer to winter travel, she relished the experience. Even when the temperature reached 54 degrees below zero, her determination was steadfast. "At no time, however, on the trip, did I suffer from cold, and so joyous and happy was I in the new experiences of winter travel, that I welcomed each hardship—and they were really few—as part of our 'great adventure.'"

The years 1913 to 1915 were a time of transition for Jobe. She had gone from expedition member to expedition leader. Like many of her mountaineering contemporaries, she began sharing her experiences with the public through lectures. She also purchased land for a camp for girls, and in 1916, after leaving Hunter College, she opened Camp Mystic.

Jobe's program catered to daughters of the wealthy, but it was no finishing school. Her goal was to teach her charges how to live in the outdoors. The girls stayed in tents, did calisthenics, rode horseback, swam, and participated in field sports like baseball, volleyball, archery, and javelin. They also went on camping trips to a nearby island. Jobe incorporated Native American culture into the curriculum, pitching a Cree tepee she had secured during her travels.

Jobe, who had succeeded in the academic world as well as in expeditions into the unknown, was an exemplary role model for the girls. She also invited friends and associates to the camp, including the husband and wife team of Martin and Osa Johnson, who filmed African wildlife; Vilhjalmur Stefansson, the Arctic explorer; and many others. Stefansson introduced her to his friend and roommate Carl Akeley, a sculptor, naturalist, explorer, and taxidermist at the American Museum of Natural History in New York. Akeley, too, received an invitation.

Carl Akeley was married to Delia (Denning) Akeley, who had struggled with him during the early years of his career, assisted him on several expeditions to Africa, and saved his life when he was attacked by an elephant. The marriage, however, had become strained. On his visits to Camp Mystic, Carl Akeley found Jobe to be attractive as well as accomplished. Jobe wore a middy and bloomers like her campers, but "even in baggy bloomers she was striking—a 'stunner,' her Mystic neighbors said." She was almost five feet nine inches, a "plucky brunette" with aristocratic features. In 1921 Carl made out his will in Mary's favor, in 1923 he and Delia were divorced, and in 1924 he and Mary were married. She was forty-six; he was sixty-eight.

When the Museum of Natural History announced its intent to send Akeley back to Africa to gather more specimens for the African Hall, Jobe took on the roles of safari manager, field assistant, and photographer. Carl and Mary began the expedition in January 1926, traveling through Kenya Colony and Tanganyika Territory to collect the plant and animal specimens that would be reassembled in lifelike portrayals of various African ecosystems. Later they would visit the Kivu volcanoes in the Belgian Congo to continue Carl's study of mountain gorillas. The trip involved drama, beauty, and hard work.

Jobe reveled in the opportunity to see this new and intriguing land. She rose each day at four thirty, breathing in the cool night air and watching the darkness as it abruptly faded. Everything beat to the tempo of the sun. As the sky grew pale, foretelling the coming burst of glory, Mary and Carl headed out to work in the grasslands and hills. The fiery sun became brighter and hotter until they were forced to retreat for the two most torrid hours of the day. They then returned to work until long after dark. The sunsets were magnificent. "The whole circle of the heavens is transformed by this most stupendous miracle of the day. Each sunset seems more beautiful than the last; and as the final act of the day's drama is done, I feel as if a curtain had been softly dropped by gracious hands upon the unfathomable mysteries of the world and all that lies beyond."

Carl declared one day that he expected Mary to give up her career and devote all her energies to his African work. Instead of being offended, Mary was gratified by the request. She was deeply devoted to her husband and his work and was pleased that he wanted her to be so involved in it. His words took on even greater importance a few weeks later as Mary and Carl were making their way to the mountains of the Congo. Carl had previously fallen ill with fever, and as they approached their research station he succumbed once more. Stormy weather had brought a hard-edged chill to the 11,000-foot camp. There in the heart of Africa Carl Akeley died, leaving Mary to face an inconceivable loss. She buried him on the mountain, grieving that their time together had been so short. "It is almost impossible for me to write of the remaining events of our Congo expedition," Mary said. "We both had felt, on the entire expedition, that life for us was only at the beginning. . . . Ultimately, I found the strength to go on alone, to complete to the best of my ability his unfinished work."

Mary accepted Carl's charge. When she returned to the United States, she took his place as adviser to the African Hall and subsequently became a member of the trustees committee on African collections. The museum named the hall, which opened in 1936, the Akeley African Hall. Mary lectured widely and wrote a series of books about Africa and Carl's work there: *Carl Akeley's Africa* (1929), *Adventures in the African Jungle* (1930), *Lions, Gorillas and Their Neighbors* (1932), and *The Restless Jungle* (1936). Mary listed Carl as the first author on two of these books.

In 1935 Mary fulfilled her childhood dream of seeing the land of the Zulu warriors when she led an expedition to study the culture of the Zulu and the Swazi in southern Africa, collect more material for the African Hall, and conduct a survey of wildlife. As early as 1929 she had spoken about the loss of wildlife: "Today the wild animals of Africa are making a losing fight. The great problem of the student of wildlife traveling in Africa today is not to defend himself against wild animals, but to actually see them." Mary's trip to southern Africa in the 1930s convinced her that both wildlife and the native people needed protection. She was among the earliest to sound the alarm.

In 1940, the same year *The Wilderness Lives Again: Carl Akeley and the Great Adventure* was published, sixty-two-year-old Mary revisited British Columbia, paddling on the Canoe River on a "journey of rediscovery" in the land of her first adventures.

As busy as she was in New York City and as much as she loved her house in Mystic, Mary still felt pulled to the wildlands of Africa. When she received an invitation from Belgium to survey wildlife in the Congo, she finished a round of author obligations attending the publication of *Rumble of a Distant Drum: A True Story of the African Hinterland* (1946), packed her safari kit, and headed across the ocean. She was sixty-eight. While in Africa she filmed great but vanishing wild animals and collected for the museum. She also made a poignant journey to Carl's grave high in the mountains, reflecting on the sorrowful day more than twenty years earlier when she had been forced to call on resources deep within her just to face each day. During the graveside visit she came down with malaria and had to be carried out in a sedan chair. She reflected on the irony that she, "whose lot throughout the years had so long been cast in the wilderness, should come to this."

Eventually, Mary retired to her home in Mystic, visiting New York and Mexico during the colder months. She had always remained aloof from the locals, and in retirement she became a recluse. She died of a stroke in 1966.

During the course of her long life Mary Jobe explored unknown lands in the Canadian northwest, introduced scores of girls to the outdoors, contributed materially to the Akeley African Hall, and raised a cry for the protection of the people and wildlife of Africa. Her legacy is one of great talent, perseverance, and courage.

My Quest in the Canadian Rockies

Our real work had just begun. Unspeakably rough, wild country lay between us and the Big Mountain [Mount Kitchie]; that we knew; how vast and how difficult, we could only conjecture. Our last hope of reaching it was to "backpack." Accordingly we took four days' provisions and our personal and climbing outfits on our backs and started into the unknown. I felt a real sadness at leaving those cayuses behind; never before had I truly realized what it meant to be a packhorse; never before had I been so tortured by a pack. Miss Springate and I each carried an eiderdown quilt, our personal belongings, and our heavy cameras—15-pound packs—while the men carried 30 to 40 pounds. We took a small shelter tent and the men had one small canvas bed-cover between them in lieu of a blanket. One frying pan, two small pails, four cups, and four spoons were the sum total of our kitchen and table outfit. I allowed myself the luxury of one cake of soap and a toothbrush, two oranges and six lemons for the climb, but a towel and a change of raiment were forbidden. It is a severe mental ordeal to make up four packs for such a trip. You are torn and distracted between the desire for warm and comfortable clothing and the distaste for carrying a heavy burden.

Securely caching our main supply of food and clothing under the big tent fly, we said good-bye to our base camp, leaving behind us on a blazed tree a legend telling of our route and destination. Soon were we plunging into alder thickets as dense as tropical jungle, and into a tangle of devil's clubs in full leaf and higher than our heads, whose thorns penetrated our thickest clothing. We forded the West Smoky easily and then struck hard climbing on the mountain beyond. From the base of the mountain ran stiff, broken cliffs of gray, weathered rocks covered with thick scrub through which we fought our way. Our packs were heavy, there was no sign of water, the heat was intense, and our progress was slow. . . .

Up, up we climbed. Noon came and passed, and still no sign of water. Flesh and blood could go no farther. Suffering with hunger, we ate our lunch, using two of our precious lemons to quench our thirst. On, on, and still no water. Finally, two hours later, near the top, we found a tiny trickling stream from which we collected a few spoonfuls of water in our rubber drinking cups. So tormenting had been my thirst, so grilling the exertion of the day, that I now expressed my feelings at finding the water in an almost incoherent babble. We climbed over a broken ridge and came out above timberline into a rock-filled amphitheater, to find that still another ridge and valley separated us from the Big Mountain. Crossing about 2 miles of rock fall, we scrambled over a long, treeless ridge and beheld without interruption the Great Ice Mountain. . . .

We donned our extra sweaters that night, stretched up the little silk fly, and slept in front of a blazing fire. As our progress in a direct line toward the mountain was now hindered by steep cliffs, we made a detour to the west through an opening in the cliffs, down an almost perpendicular wall, well forested with rhododendrons and devil's clubs. Here we reached the valley of the big glacial river, the Big Salmon, with its three converging branches which draw their headwaters from large glaciers on the northeast side of the Big Mountain.

This additional day consumed in reaching the base of the mountain put us on short rations. One large "flapjack," without butter or sugar, was our luncheon allowance. It was amazing how that flapjack cheered us and stayed us during the six and one-half hours of our afternoon's march. We exulted over the glorious landscape and over our goal so near. Here was beauty and wildness and experience enough for a year's contemplation.

We intended to camp on the terminal moraine of the east glacier, for it runs into the timber, where it would have been easy to obtain fuel. However, an approaching thunderstorm made camp a necessity when we were about a mile below the moraine. We barely got the little silk shelter-tent up and our packs and some dry balsam boughs inside when the storm broke. All night the rain and snow fell. The next day was an impossible one for climbing. . . .

[On the day following,] just as we reached this second glacier the big, ashy-gray snow clouds broke in a rage over us. Pulling on our extra sweaters, mittens, and caps against the wind, we huddled close to the rocks, gasping for breath, and watched the storm hurl itself on the valley below. Now the view of the flowing glacier and the southern ridge shifted and changed like a kaleidoscope. First the clouds rent themselves on the shaggy heads of the big towers and enveloped their lower cliffs in mist and in straight spikes of sleety rain; below that the clouds drifted down, down to where crawled the jade-green glacier into a vista of black woods with wild branches beating under the fury of the storm. All around us were sleet and snow and the voice of the avalanche calling from peak to peak. . . .

My ice-encrusted clothing was stiff like a coat of armor, my hands were so wet and paralyzed that I could scarcely grip my ice ax, and my benumbed feet were heavy and unsteady in snow-clogged boots. The north wind groaned and howled because it was so miserable, and I groaned because I was unable even to catch a glimpse of the north side of the Big Mountain. I knew that our diminished "grub pile" made the possibility of another attempt doubtful, and the thought of failure made me sick and unhappy. However, there are four conditions in climbing when it is best for one to agree swiftly with the laws of nature. A blizzard heads the list. Never argue with a snowstorm at 7,000 feet above sea level! Give it up and wait for a fair day! With the storm still breaking over us, we picked our way cautiously and haltingly over the crevasse-filled ice, and ten hours after our start reached camp, drenched to the skin. As backpacking does not allow the luxury of a change of raiment, we dried out by the fire. We were now on very short rations [and had to turn back].

The return trip through rain-soaked underbrush was melancholy. I was aware only of rain—freezing, drenching rain that penetrated every fiber of my clothing, and of the treacherous muskeg into which I repeatedly fell.

The noon came with regal sunshine, tempered by a breeze that drove the clouds in drifts across the sky and revealed the Big Mountain clear against a dark-blue vault. It was bad enough to give up our climb in the face of foul weather; but it was infinitely worse to turn our backs upon our hearts' desire now that it had cleared, and all for the lack of a little food. After a most meager lunch of one piece of bannock and a thin slice of bacon, and tea all around, we had remaining only flour enough for two small bannocks, some tea, two lemons, and four slices of bacon.

I was heartsick with disappointment. "There was a tear in every word you spoke that first day on the home trip," Phillips confided to me afterward. . . .

[After securing a caribou for meat] a second attack on the Big Mountain was now assured. However, as Wilkins had developed rheumatism in his shoulder, it was decided that he should return to the main camp. Miss Springate had not attempted to climb on the previous trip, and now, although keen for the experience of a second expedition to the base of the mountain, she graciously abandoned any idea of going back when she realized that it would be impossible for Phillips to pack supplies for three. It was this unselfish act which makes possible the rest of this story.

Phillips and I accordingly returned to our old camp, having cut down our packs to the last ounce. We took with us the four slices of bacon and some of the tea and flour, but our main food supply was the freshly killed caribou. We had no salt. Instead of carrying the silk shelter-tent, we strung up the piece of canvas as a windbreak and slept by the fire.

A camp in the mountains at snowline and without any shelter to speak of is not a pleasant thing to contemplate. The wind howls down the mountainside and chills you through and through; the fire demands serious and constant attention, burning out and having to be replenished before you are properly warmed. The night is interminable.

At daybreak we began our climb, following our old route across the east glacier, over the long moraine, and thence across the cliffs to the second glacier. Going beyond the point at which the storm had driven us back, we found the second glacier of vast extent, very steep, and deeply serrated with crevasses, some of them 20 feet in width and easily 50 feet in depth. On either side of us were great ice walls, 500 to 1,000 feet high, blue and crevassed from foot to top. As far as the eye could range forward were long vistas of snow, huge boulder-like lumps of ice, stretches of deep crevasses opening into the very bowels of the glacier ice with shallow spanning snow bridges of glaring, staring white.

Crossing about 5 miles of ice, we at last reached a long sloping shoulder where our aneroid registered 7,800 feet. We were immediately under the northwest face of the main peak. "What do you think of it now?" Phillips called out, as he paused a moment in his step cutting. "I can't see anything but my feet," I replied. I was struggling up the last stiff bit of ice. A few more steps and I stood in a new world, somewhere between earth and heaven. A huge ice peak, sheer and terrible, rose straight in front of me. From the base the eye traveled up a steep snow slope to perpendicular rock cliffs, deeply notched with chimneys; it traveled from ice field to higher cliffs, more formidable than those below, and at last rested on the cold blue of an austere mountaintop, a pile of broken ice and demolished snow cornices. Through the glasses the ice cap appeared like a deeply crevassed glacier with a wilderness of *seracs* upheaved to a vertical position, filled with great blue-green ice grottoes. Icicles 50 feet long depended across these caves. The *arête* was everywhere broken and knifelike.

"I'd rather take you up Mt. Robson twice," was Phillips's only comment.

Confirming our experience of all the slopes on the entire trip, this northwest face was the most formidable of all. As I looked, the great ice field above us was rent by a mad avalanche, which plunged down over the rock cliffs directly in our path. The sight of it was overwhelming. The mountain was obviously impossible to our two selves with our limited equipment. . . .

We could easily have climbed some 800 feet farther, but as that would have been futile, we built a cairn at 7,500 feet and returned to our camp after having spent fourteen hours on the mountain.

When night fell upon our little moraine wickiup and the white glacial mist whipped down upon us, I felt as if I had left my conscious self somewhere upon the mountaintop. I scarcely recognized myself—a battered, grimy creature crouching by the dimming fire. I was too weary even to unlace my boots. Phillips looked at me curiously.

"You are dead tired; and—you're as dirty as a man," he said.

On the home trail I could scarcely drag one foot after the other. The unvaried diet of unsalted caribou was palling upon me. I was growing desperately weak. I would have given my birthright for a pinch of salt. The absurdity of the situation was the quantity of meat we consumed and our perpetual hunger. At lunch we greedily ate 5 pounds of deliciously tender steak, broiled over hot coals, and an hour afterward we were hungrier than before. The charred fat alone satisfied us.

All day I was conscious that my pace was being carefully watched, and my pack was lightened until I was ashamed. We rested often as we dared, for we had promised the others we would be back at the horse camp on the fourth day. We camped at the foot of the rhododendron hill. "It's too much for you today," Phillips had said. "You get a good long rest tonight, and tomorrow you'll go up like an aeroplane." But I didn't. It was afternoon before we got to Providence Pass. I was growing increasingly weary and weak.

Across the treeless pass we struck four hours of good going. "If we can get down to the river at six-thirty, we can eat supper in camp tonight," Phillips had cheered me on. Below treeline we found quantities of huckleberries, which we ate like bears. We reached the West Smoky at six-thirty. Here it was a tearing torrent 200 feet wide that ran clear as crystal over blue and red and green boulders. "You waded that like a moose," was my reward. I was on my last wind. We were more than two hours from camp, with 1,500 feet of climbing through windfalls, rhododendrons and devil's clubs ahead of us. Troubled lest darkness overtake us, I marched ahead, putting all my strength in this final spurt. It was not enough! My water-filled boots retarded me at every step. I fell in my tracks when we stopped to rest. Presently I was stumbling and falling just because my feet would not coordinate. Up over ledges of rock, through rhododendrons and devil's clubs and rhododendrons again, we climbed until we came to a long windfall and to slippery rocks beyond which the darkness lay. My pack was crushing my shoulders. The devil's clubs were lacerating my face and arms. Although Phillips kept not more than 20 feet ahead of me, I could scarcely see him, it was so dark. Soon, I could only hear him. I floundered on, falling again and again over logs and into holes, and sinking sometimes to earth merely because of my own weight. Once when I hit my knee a stinging blow on a sharp stake, and did not get up immediately, Phillips heard me groan and started back toward me. I lurched up before he could reach my side. He went on and mercifully said nothing. I was desperately afraid that my voice might grow unsteady.

I now began to use every sort of mental lash I could command. "You *must* get into camp tonight or Miss Springate will think you are at the bottom of a crevasse." "Go on now; don't go to pieces at the finish." "See; it is easy to take one step; you can take another." And, "It would be a disgraceful thing to sit down and weep." So I goaded myself up the hill.

Phillips said: "Don't worry; you can't lose the old man in the dark. We'll come out in that open place below the camp." And we did, marvelously guided by the most unerring brain I have ever known on the trail.

A half-hour below camp we shouted, and heard an answering call. They had been hallooing all afternoon, expecting our early return. We made camp at nine o'clock.

Our entrance into camp that night was one of the intensest moments of my life. They had greeting and cheer and warmth for us; we had the story of our climb for them. Safe, dry-clad, and satisfied in the shelter of the base camp, I now realized, for the first time, that we had taken long chances, but we had explored "Kitchi," the Big Mountain.

Marion Randall Parsons with her husband (left) and another Sierra Club camper.

9

DWELLING CLOSE TO THE HEART OF THINGS

Marion Randall Parsons

(1880–1953)

We reached the rocks at last, but not until every ray of daylight was gone. The young moon, from which we had expected some assistance, was hidden behind the mountain, and though its light could be dimly perceived on the distant landscape below us, we were in shadow, in almost complete darkness. While we stood there, shivering, hungry, inexpressibly weary in body, and in mind almost despairing of ever reaching shelter that night, two lights flickered up, far, far below— beacon fires that our comrades had kindled to help us find the way.

In her many years of mountaineering Marion Randall Parsons climbed over fifty high peaks—from the Sierras, Cascades, and Olympics to the Selkirks, Canadian Rockies, and Alps. She climbed not for fame but for pleasure. She relished the physical challenge of ascents as well as the moments of solitude, time spent with friends, and the spectacular scenery. In the mountains she found a simplicity and an intensity of life that she found nowhere else.

Parsons was introduced to mountaineering by Wanda Muir, John Muir's older daughter. A shy, home-schooled, twenty-two-year-old, Parsons donned a heavy denim hiking skirt that fell to a few inches below her knee and joined a month-long Sierra Club campout in the mountains. She was awestruck by the beauty of the Sierras. She made dozens of new friends, found muscles she had not known she had, and discovered that she loved the outdoors.

"For a little while," she wrote of that first trip, "you have dwelt close to the heart of things. You have lain down to sleep in a wide chamber walled about by mountains rising darkly against the lesser darkness of the sky, where stars looked down on you between the pines, stars more brilliant than on the frostiest night in the lowland; you have awakened to the laughter of streams and the songs of birds." This trip and others that followed profoundly affected Parsons. "These things live with you long after the outing has passed and you are back in the working world. . . . [They become] your strength, your inspiration, and some of the brightest hours you have ever lived."

On the 1903 trip Marion not only developed a keenness for life and a deep and abiding love of the mountains, but she also met Edward Taylor Parsons, a founder and director of the Sierra Club, whom she described as "the aristocrat of good-fellowship." E. T. was impressed with the energy and contributions women provided to the Sierra Club's high trips, saying that "their vigor and endurance [are] a revelation to all of us." When Marion appeared he was more than impressed; the two were married four years later and had seven years together.

During this time Parsons wrote about several trips, including one to Mount Saint Helens, a peak in south-central Washington, in 1909 (see "On Mt. St. Helens with the Mazamas," following). The trip was organized by the Mazamas, a hiking group based in Portland, Oregon. Packhorses transported gear to the next-to-last camp, and then the men carried food and blankets to the base camp. But the group started late, and the ascent took longer than planned; eight of the thirty-six members of the party turned back because of dwindling time. Marion was among those who continued. Her account describes the trials and tense moments the dauntless crew met in trying to attain its goal.

In 1914 E. T. died, and Parsons faced the inevitable question, what next? Despite her uncertainty about the future, two elements of her life remained steadfast: her need to find solitude and adventure in the mountains and her enthusiasm for the Sierra Club. Like Mary Jobe Akeley, she stepped into her husband's shoes and carried on his work. Parsons was elected to succeed E. T. as a director of the Sierra Club, becoming the first woman to serve on the board. Over time, her involvement with the Sierra Club helped to give her life the direction and focus she needed, and she continued as a director for over twenty years. She was the club's treasurer from 1915 to 1919, and she served on the advisory board of, and wrote many articles for, the *Sierra Club Bulletin* through the late 1940s.

In addition to her involvement with the club, she began to help John Muir organize notes for his book *Travels in Alaska*. The project provided a welcome diversion after E. T.'s death, and Muir needed the help. "Confusion was no word for the state of the manuscripts," Parsons observed. "The arrangement proved unexpectedly happy and congenial to us both, and lasted until within a week of his death [in late 1914]." She then prepared the manuscript for publication; it was, wrote Muir's biographer, William Badè, "a task to which she brought devotion as well as ability."

Parsons's work allowed her to explore and enjoy her other interest, mountaineering. In June 1915 Parsons and three friends planned a "knapsacking" trip through Yosemite with the goal of climbing Mount Clark, a high peak in the Merced group. They were pushing the season, though, and encountered snow and ice en route. Without a rope or ice axes they could not proceed, and reluctantly the four turned back to their camp in Yosemite Valley. Parson's account of this trip, "A Woman's Tramping Trip Through Yosemite," addresses some questions that might have been asked of early backpackers:

> We women who "knapsack" pride ourselves on being able to do our share—so while we do not pretend to carry such heavy packs as the men, we carry our own outfits and a part, at least, of the general commissary supplies. Short-skirted, flannel-shirted, with hob-nailed boots to the knee and "shocking bad hats," we are as easy in our own clothing and as regardless of wind or weather as the men themselves.
>
> It was rather hard for us to nerve ourselves to meet the stares and queries of the tourists we met along the valley trail over which our trip must begin. All the way up to Little Yosemite we were beset with questions: Where were we going? Didn't we find it very hard work? Wouldn't we get lost? Weren't we afraid of getting sunburned? We had an inclination to slink shamefacedly by these proper-looking folk.

Parsons also describes a simplicity of camping that has virtually been lost today:

> Our personal outfits, of course, were reduced to bare essentials. A sleeping bag, weighing about eight pounds, a sweater, a change of hose, toothbrush, hairbrush, towel, a box of matches, and a tiny roll of adhesive tape would about complete the list. Tin buckets, a small frying pan and a tin cup and spoon apiece comprised the camp equipment. . . . A knapsacker's camp is a simple affair—a bed of pine needles, a

few stones rolled together to make a fireplace, a pile of firewood gathered together; and there is home.

Later that summer she set out with Lulie Nettleton, E. W. Harnden, and Dave Brown for the Selkirks in British Columbia. There the party made the first ascent of a peak they called Mount Bruce, which they estimated to be 11,000 feet high. In 1915 Parsons was elected to membership in the American Alpine Club. Her mountaineering résumé included Whitney, Lyell, Dana, Ritter, South Kaweah, Conness, Parker, Mammoth, North Peak, and Parsons in the Sierra Nevada, plus a complete traverse of Tuolumne Canyon; Rainier, Shasta, Mount Saint Helens, Baker, South Sister, and Glacier Peak in the Cascades; Olympus and Seattle in the Olympics; and Mount Bruce in the Purcell Range. The list was impressive for a woman who had gone on her first camping trip in the mountains only thirteen years earlier.

Some of the women profiled in this book, such as Annie Peck and Mary Roberts Rinehart, craved public acclamation; others, like Dora Keen, were thrust briefly into the spotlight. Although Parsons wrote often for the *Sierra Club Bulletin* and other publications and in doing so showed quietly that women could partake of and enjoy knapsacking, she was essentially a private person. She was willing to write trip accounts, but she shared in print little else of her life.

A careful reading of her trip articles does, however, reveal Parsons's appreciation for the natural world and the insights she garnered there:

But there is perhaps no day quite so perfect as that which holds this hint of coming change. Even a sunny April morning with all its wealth of blossoms and riot of bird songs lacks something of the charm of that hour when winter's hold is first loosened and the coming of spring heralded. For change and growth are intrinsic parts of the beauty of nature, and one secret of its deep appeal to us is this abounding promise of new life ever hastening to succeed the old, this radiant spirit of eternal youth that touches most closely the strongest, deepest instincts of our race.

In summer 1917 Parsons and Nettleton set out for the Canadian Rockies. They took the ferry north from Seattle and the train east from Prince Rupert, arriving at Robson Station near Mount Robson in British Columbia. They considered a horseback trip to Maligne Lake but decided to climb instead, hiring Donald Phillips as their guide. (Mary Jobe had hired Phillips as a guide in 1914 and 1915 and would travel with him in the winter of 1917.)

Parsons fantasized about attempting Mount Robson: "I had dreamed of climbing it, of course; had pictured myself standing on its snowy summit after hours of superhuman toil; had even in my mind's eye seen the Sunday supplements with pictures of me hanging over a precipice at one end of a rope while a Swiss guide with a feather in his cap clung to the other." But when the two women got a good look at Robson and its "cruel and formidable" countenance, they decided Robson "was no mountain for women to climb—not for two women with only one [guide] at any rate." Instead, they ascended 10,000-foot Mount Pam, from which they could see Mount Kitchie on the horizon.

Parsons's climbing adventures were interrupted by World War I, when she began working with the Civilian Relief section of the American Red Cross in France. In August 1918 she took charge of relief efforts for refugees in Landes and then worked in Ardennes until July 1919. Both the Red Cross and the French government honored Parsons for her work. But she was eager to return to the mountains, as her article about the 1920 Sierra Club trip to the headwaters of the San Joaquin and the Kings in the Sierra reveals: "It was like old times in the Sierra Club." She also wrote accounts of a personal trip to the Austrian and Italian Alps in 1925 and of a 1929 Sierra Club high trip along the John Muir Trail from the South Fork of the San Joaquin River to Tuolumne Meadows in Yosemite.

On the 1929 trip Parsons traveled with other Sierra Club veterans, people like Will Colby (a leader within the club) and Virginia and Ansel Adams. She was almost fifty and felt the bittersweet passage of time: "We still tread the mountain trails, it is true, and flatter ourselves that we will continue to do so yet for many a year. We still climb the passes and lay siege to the lesser peaks; but the days of highest rapture, the real climbing days, the more arduous knapsacking days, become fewer and fewer, and soon necessarily must be past."

Parsons noted the ways clothing had evolved. On her first trip she had worn a denim skirt with a hem that reached below her knees. Women on the 1929 trip wore "shorties" and "sun backs," prompting much controversy among those on the trip. Some of the more conservative participants called the younger hikers "nudes." Parsons, remembering the disparaging remarks people had made about her and her women friends when they had worn knickerbockers, wryly observed that judgment should be passed through the healthy lens of perspective.

Parsons also recognized that the Sierrans had made progress in protecting the mountains by bringing those areas to public attention and working to limit grazing. But that attention also caused degradation—more people, parking lots, campgrounds, and trails—a paradox that continues to trouble conservationists to this day.

A few years later Parsons was confined to bed with a serious illness, and it became clear that her knapsacking days were over. Still hungering for adventure, she was left to pursue it on milder terms. She had written several novels in the 1920s, and in the 1930s she taught herself to paint, often portraying the high mountains she loved so well. She continued with this work until she died in Berkeley, California, in 1953.

The mountaineering world has little noted people such as Marion Randall Parsons who made no spectacular first ascents and recorded no death-defying feats. Parsons hiked and climbed quietly. She was at home in the mountains and reported on her trips in straightforward, unembellished language. She would not have said, as did Mary Roberts Rinehart, that she was "dying" en route to a summit. Mountaineering involved hard work. The point was not to focus on tired muscles but on the many opportunities the mountains had to offer: time with friends, time alone, time with nature to work out one's place there, and time to follow one's inner yearning for adventure.

On Mt. St. Helens with the Mazamas

Our camp was made in the shelter of the highest timber, if timber it could be called, that was little more than shrubbery, high on the bleak mountainside in a little depression where the winds that blew off the snow could in some measure pass over our heads. Blazing fires, supper, and an hour of storytelling brought us cheerfully to bedtime, when we lay watching the brilliant stars and the dim outline of the mountain against the sky until we fell asleep. Little did we guess then what our next night['s] impression of St. Helens would be!

We arose at five next morning, but there was some delay in starting, and we were not on the march 'til past seven. A little above camp we dropped into the floor of one of the numerous glacial cañons by which the mountain is furrowed, and by means of it approached the first snow slope. Before we had fairly begun to climb, the sun, whose earliest rays had reached the northern slope, had so far softened the snow that it made slow, difficult going. Nor was this the worst. On St. Helens the arms of rock that extend into the snow are composed of lava boulders loosely imbedded in pumice. Wherever rock and snow meet, the action of the sun sends cannonades of rocks down upon the slopes below. We were seldom out of range of this bombardment. Fortunately the rocks that fell were small and scattered, and the snow was seldom so steep that we could not dodge; but the thought of the havoc that might be wrought in our ranks should the mountain choose to let loose the full strength of its batteries scarcely added to the pleasure of the climb. We encountered no dangerous work on the lower part of the mountain, but twice the crossing of crevasses consumed so much valuable time in the adjustment of alpenstocks and ropes that it was not until two o'clock that we reached the top of the "Lizard" and paused for lunch.

The Lizard is a long promontory of rocks, a divide between two glaciers. Its tail loses itself in the lower pumice slopes, while its head stretched far upward, two-thirds of the way to the summit. It was our first opportunity to fairly gauge our rate of progress—hardly an encouraging one in view of the steeper climbing that must lay ahead. This was the time, of course, for us to acknowledge our defeat and turn back to make a better start some other day, but to give up was the last thought in the minds of most of us. Eight of the party did wisely determine to return, but the rest of us, in the cheerful optimism of halfway up, thought we might "if we tried" reach the summit by four-thirty.

However, there was still a long snowfield to be traversed, still another rocky promontory to be climbed, and it was close upon five o'clock before we reached the foot of the final steep ice slope that guards the summit. Here it was necessary to cut steps and to use the rope, and although the difficult place was short, probably not more than 200 or 300 feet, our progress had to be slow. At last we reached the top of the ice, climbed a little rocky eminence, and emerged upon the broad snowfield that crowns St. Helens. The true summit lies at the southwestern extremity of this field, so we crossed it and at 7:15 attained the highest point.

Today, as we who stood there recall the scene, memory assures us that it was one of the most impressive and beautiful that our eyes had ever met. For hundreds of miles the forest country lay stretched at our feet, dark and shadowy and half veiled in mist. Westward the great red sun, vanishing in a

MARION RANDALL PARSONS

rosy glow of fog, seemed also at our feet, so far were we set above the sea and its dim horizon line. The sky was bright with rose and yellow and palest green. North, east, and south of us the three great snow cones—Rainier, Adams, and Hood—were so aglow with sunset light that it seemed as if lingering flames must still burn on these altars of ancient fires. Before their glory was gone night had closed in upon the lowlands. The winds of the daytime were stilled and the silence of the high places was upon us. The lowland nights are full of sound, a thousand wee rustlings and whisperings and flittings of unseen winged creatures, the stir of leaf, the tinkling drop of water; but in the white lands when night comes all is silence, a silence significant not of death, but rather of the unborn ages yet to come.

All this we can remember now, but at the moment the wonder of it was almost lost in the sense of loneliness, of vastness, of piercing cold. That enormous bulk of ice, snow, and treacherous rock separating us from fire, water, food, and the haunts of man was all that our minds could con-sciously grasp. We rested only long enough to register our names and to elect to membership in the Mazama Club those who had qualified by the ascent. Short as the delay was, our captain was already impatiently calling us to hurry. The bitter cold, too, gave scant encouragement to loiterers, so we hastened to start on the descent.

It has been asked why we did not choose the less haz-ardous experience of remaining on the summit all night. We might have more safely done so, indeed, had we been better equipped for it; but some of us were without sweaters or coats, our feet were soaking wet and almost numb with cold, and we were without food. With several rather delicate women and one boy of twelve in the party, the risk of expo-sure was deemed too great.

The sun was now quite out of sight and a chill gray twilight was creeping up the glacial cañon from the darker wooded valleys. As we stood on the brink of the ice slope the last gleam of color faded from the distant mountains. A luminous, winding band of silver, marking the course of the Toutle River, still shone in the dark forest to westward, but all else was gray and cold, desolate and forbidding.

We were placed in line, alternately, a man and a woman, and the rope stretched between us with the caution not to grasp it except in case of a slip, but to pass it lightly through our hands. It was fastened at the upper end to two alpenstocks which were planted as securely as possible in the ice and were held by a strong man. Two men then went ahead with ice axes, with which they enlarged the steps we had used on the ascent, for the surface of the ice was now so hard frozen and slippery that every change of position had to be made with the utmost care. The step makers went forward to the end of our 50 feet of rope, and then the signal was given for us to advance. Facing the mountain, alpenstock in one hand, rope in the other, we went down backward as on a ladder, one step at a time, as far as the line would permit. Then we halted. The last man followed, holding the end of the rope, planted it again, the step makers went forward, and again we advanced six or eight steps. Sixteen times the rope was shifted in this manner, and sixteen times we stood for five or more minutes motionless in the freezing cold, our hands and feet so numb that it seemed almost impossible to move when the signal to change position was given.

It was fortunate that all of us were not equally aware of the gravity of the situation. The rope, insufficiently secured as it was, could not have borne much strain, and, as our company was largely composed of tenderfeet, there was among us scarcely one in five who knew how to save himself from the consequences of a slip on the easiest snow slope, much less on the glassy, steep surface of that ice. Had some of the novices realized how easily a single misstep could have precipitated one or more of us into the cruel pile of rocks that lay so far below, an attack of unreasoning panic might have brought about that very catastrophe. That no accident did occur is due in great measure to the cool, unhurried, confident manner of our leaders, to whose work that night too high praise cannot be accorded.

We reached the rocks at last, but not until every ray of daylight was gone. The young moon, from which we had expected some assistance, was hidden behind the mountain, and though its light could be dimly perceived on the distant landscape below us, we were in shadow, in almost complete darkness. While we stood there, shivering, hungry, inexpressibly weary in body, and in mind almost despairing of ever reaching shelter that night, two lights flickered up, far, far below—beacon fires that our comrades had kindled to help us find the way. It is difficult to describe what hope and encouragement those two little friendly gleams put into our hearts. They typified the warmth and sympathy of human fellowship as against the merciless indifference that nature in her sterner moods shows to the needs, even to the lives, of men.

Our way now for awhile led down a rocky crest, composed, like much of St. Helens, of large, easily detached boulders set among smaller rocks and loose pumice. We formed in a close phalanx, two and two, a man and a woman, with the rope between us. Walking as near together as possible, we moved slowly forward. If a large rock showed signs of starting we threw our united weight against it, and either stopped it or deflected it to one side, where it could roll its course to the foot of the mountain, if need be, without harming us. The detonations of these crashing rocks, the crunch of our marching feet, and the flash of steel caulks on the stones remain vivid recollections of this part of the descent.

A rock slide was the next incident. Such great quantities of rock were displaced with each step that it was judged wisest to cross this only two at a time. By holding hands and keeping the step the transit was made safely, though with a tremendous accompaniment of rolling stones. We emerged from this on the snow, fortunately a deeply furrowed and not very steep field, which brought us to the top of the Lizard. So far we had been following our course of the afternoon, but here, instead of descending to the snowfields on the right from which we had made the ascent, we concluded to keep on down the Lizard to avoid if possible the steeper snow, which, in its frozen condition, would be very dangerous. The Lizard's backbone was composed of less formidable boulders than we had encountered near the summit, but even these smaller missiles became objects of terror in the darkness, especially as, owing to the delay on the rock slide, the party had become scattered and it was impossible to know in what direction danger lay. The cry of "Rock coming!" was so frequent and was attended by such breathless moments of suspense—ears trying to locate the ominous crashing, eyes straining the blackness in a vain attempt to see the threatening object—that for many a night afterward we were haunted by it in our dreams.

Once we followed the wrong arm of rock and found ourselves blocked at the end by a network of crevasses. Here, at the urgent request of a distant voice from the snowfield, we sat fast for ten minutes holding the rocks down until the explorer below was out of range before we could retrace our way and climb up to the western arm. The campfires were growing closer now, but there was still another rock ordeal to pass through, a narrow chimney leading from the Lizard to a snowfield, nearly all of the upper part of which was within range of the chimney. This, however, was the last of the rock bombardment, indeed the last difficulty of the descent, for the snowfield led by an easy grade to the edge of the pumice slope.

At two o'clock in the morning, nineteen hours after we had left it, our stumbling feet brought us to the temporary camp, with its great fire, its steaming cups of chocolate, its bread and meat, and the greatest blessing of all, its sleeping bags, into which we straightway tumbled without even the ceremony of removing the grease paint from our faces.

We were none of us the worse for the experience next day. On the contrary, we awoke with a sense of exhilaration. The sun seemed to shine with a more cordial warmth and the joy of being alive on good old Mother Earth was a little keener than on an everyday morning. We were a little disposed to philosophize on the comforts of the commonplace and the folly of seeking to attain high summits, but we were exceedingly glad to have been there just the same.

The few remaining days of the outing sped pleasantly, though the eve of our departure brought the rain which had fortunately spared us so far. The final day and night in camp passed in that jumble of discomfort and hilarity which storms generally produce in camp, provided the elements have been considerate enough to reserve their bad behavior for the last days, when good fellowship is at its height and a certain jaunty indifference to cold, wet, and such extraneous matters has become the criterion of one's position in the social economy of camp life.

And then came the breaking of camp, and we followed the homeward road through the forests to find that while we had been on the heights autumn had been busy with the low country woods. For on every maple and dogwood were painted her warning signs, telling us that it was time to leave the summer country and go back to the world of roofs again.

APPENDIX: CHRONOLOGY

Women's firsts and major world events (in italic) and major points in the lives of women in *Adventurous Women*.

1840s

1840   Martha F. Whitman is born on July 13 to Mary (Fairfield) Whitman and Jason Whitman in Portland, Maine.

1841   *The first university degrees are awarded to American women.*

1848   *The first women's rights convention is held at Seneca Falls, New York; Elizabeth Gerritt (Smith) Miller wears pantalettes.*

     The New England Female Medical College, the first medical school for women, is founded.

1849   *Elizabeth Blackwell is the first woman to earn a medical degree in the United States.*

1850s

1850   Annie S. Peck is born on October 19 to Ann Power (Smith) Peck and George Bachelder Peck in Providence, Rhode Island.

1851   *Amelia Bloomer, a writer and editor, advocates reform in women's clothing, popularizing the pantalettes (from then on called bloomers) worn at Seneca.*

1858   *Julia Archibald Homes climbs Pikes Peak in Colorado.*

1860s

1861   *The U.S. Civil War begins.*

1862   E. Pauline Johnson is born on March 10 to Emily Susanna (Howells) Johnson and George Henry Martin Johnson in Brantford, Ontario.

| 1869 | *The National Woman Suffrage Association (NWSA) and the American Woman Suffrage Association (AWSA) are organized.* |

1870s

| 1870s | Martha F. Whitman camps in the White Mountains and climbs Mount Washington during a storm. |

| 1871 | Dora Keen is born on June 24 to E. Corinna (Borden) Keen and William W. Keen in Philadelphia, Pennsylvania. |

Britain's Lucy Walker makes the first ascent of the Matterhorn by a woman (the first male ascent occurred in 1865).

| 1872 | Grace Gallatin is born on January 28 to Clemenzia (Rhodes) Gallatin and Albert Gallatin in Sacramento, California. |

| 1873 | *Britain's Isabella Bird climbs Longs Peak in Colorado.* |

Boston University takes over the New England Female Medical College and the program becomes coeducational.

| 1876 | Elinore Pruitt is born on June 3 to Josephine (Courtney) Pruitt and Mr. Pruitt (first name unknown) in Indian Territory (now Oklahoma). |

Mary Ella Roberts is born on August 12 to Cornelia (Gilleland) Roberts and Tom Roberts in Pittsburgh, Pennsylvania.

The Appalachian Mountain Club is formed; members vote to admit women.

Martha Whitman joins the Appalachian Mountain Club.

| 1877 | *In her book* Question of Rest for Women During Menstruation, *physician Mary Putnam challenges the belief that women should refrain from normal activities during their menstrual cycle.* |

| 1878 | Annie Peck graduates from the University of Michigan, earning honors in every subject. |

Mary Jobe is born on January 29 to Sarah Jane (Pittis) Jobe and Richard Watson Jobe in Tappan, Ohio.

1880s

1880   Marion Randall is born on December 14 to Nancy (Garabrant) Randall and Charles Randall in San Francisco, California.

1880s   Martha Whitman continues to hike in the White Mountains of New Hampshire.

     Elinore Pruitt briefly attends grade school.

1881   Annie Peck receives a masters degree from the University of Michigan.

1884   Martha Whitman graduates from Boston University School of Medicine, sets up a practice, and dies from typhoid fever.

1885   Annie Peck is the first woman to attend the American School of Classical Studies in Athens.

1889   *The "safety" bicycle is introduced in the United States, making bicycling more available to women as well as men; within four years over a million Americans are riding these bicycles.*

1890s

1890   *Fay Fuller is the first woman to climb Mount Rainier in Washington.*

     The two major suffrage organizations merge to form the National American Woman Suffrage Association.

1890s   Mary Roberts receives—and rides—the second girl's bicycle in Philadelphia; neighbors protest that bicycling is immodest and improper for a girl.

     Pauline Johnson tours Canada, England, and the United States giving recitals of what she calls her Indian poems.

1891	*Outing* magazine publishes Pauline Johnson's "Ripples and Paddle Plashes."
1892	Pauline Johnson writes her most famous poem, "The Song My Paddle Sings."
	The Sierra Club is founded; six women are among the charter members.
1893–1894	Elinore Pruitt's mother and stepfather die, leaving Elinore, at age eighteen, in charge of five siblings.
1895	Annie Peck, wearing knickerbockers, becomes the third woman to climb the Matterhorn.
1896	Mary Roberts graduates from nursing school and marries Dr. Stanley Rinehart.
	Dora Keen graduates from Bryn Mawr.
	Grace Gallatin marries Ernest Thompson Seton.
1897	Mary Jobe graduates from Scio (later Mt. Union) College.
	Grace Gallatin Seton embarks on her first wildlife and camping trip; she later writes about the trip in *A Woman Tenderfoot*, published in the United States in 1905.

1900s

1900	Annie Peck attends the Congrès International de l'Alpinisme in Paris as a U.S. delegate.
	Wyoming joins the union; its constitution is the first to grant women the right to vote.
1902	At about this time Elinore Pruitt marries Harry Rupert, and they file on a homestead in Oklahoma Territory.
1903	Marion Randall, at the urging of Wanda Muir, signs up for her first Sierra Club outing; Randall continues to go on trips with the Sierra Club and other organizations for thirty years.

1903–1906	Annie Peck attempts to reach the summit of various peaks in South America.
1905	Elinore Pruitt Rupert and her husband are divorced.
	Mary Jobe and college friends (who collectively call themselves the Selkirk Pathfinders) spend three months in British Columbia, Canada.
	"Suffragette" is used in print for the first time.
1906	*Fanny Bullock Workman, a feminist, sets an altitude record for women when she climbs 22,810-foot Pinnacle Peak in India.*
1907	Marion Randall marries Edward T. Parsons, a founder and director of the Sierra Club.
	Grace Gallatin Seton's second book, *Nimrod's Wife*, is published.
1908	At age fifty-eight, Annie Peck makes the first ascent of the North Peak of Huascaran in Peru and believes she may have set an altitude record for women. In fact, she only gains the record for the highest altitude in the Western Hemisphere, as the peak is eventually measured at 21,812 feet.
	Mary Roberts Rinehart's first book, *The Circular Staircase*, establishes the genre of humorous detective novel; she becomes one of the most highly paid writers of her time.
1909	Elinore Pruitt Rupert files on a homestead in southwestern Wyoming and marries Clyde Stewart.
	Dora Keen reaches the summit of the Matterhorn and the summits of nine other peaks in the Swiss Alps.

1910s

1910	Dora Keen reaches the summit of Mount Blanc and summits of six other peaks in the French Alps.

1910–1912	Grace Gallatin Seton helps to establish the Camp Fire Girls.
1910–1920	Grace Gallatin Seton serves as a leader in the women's suffrage movement.
1911	Annie Peck makes the first ascent of Mount Coropuna in Peru, planting at the summit a flag proclaiming "Votes for Women."
	Dora Keen makes her first attempt on Mount Blackburn in Alaska.
1912	Dora Keen succeeds in climbing Mount Blackburn.
	Girl Guides (later Girl Scouts of America) is founded.
1913	Pauline Johnson dies at age fifty-one.
	Willa Cather's Oh Pioneers! *celebrates life on the prairie.*
1913–1914	Elinore Pruitt Stewart's letters are published in *Atlantic Monthly* and as a book, *Letters of a Woman Homesteader.*
1914	Dora Keen makes scientific observations of Alaskan glaciers.
	Marion Randall Parsons's husband dies, and she succeeds him on the board of the Sierra Club, becoming the first woman director; she serves for twenty-two years.
	Parsons assists John Muir in the preparation of *Travels in Alaska* before his death in December.
	Archduke Ferdinand is assassinated, precipitating World War I.
	A woman designs and takes out a patent on an elastic brassiere.
	Margaret Sanger uses the term birth control *in her writings.*
1914–1915	Mary Jobe makes several attempts to climb Mount Sir Alexander in the Canadian Rockies.

1915	Marion Randall Parsons and three companions make the first ascent of Mount Bruce in the Purcell Range. Parsons is elected to the American Alpine Club; she has climbed peaks in the Sierra Nevada, Cascades, Olympics, and Purcell Range.
	Elinore Pruitt Stewart's second set of letters is published in *Atlantic Monthly* and as a book, *Letters on an Elk Hunt*.
	Mary Roberts Rinehart goes to Europe to cover the war; she is the first reporter (male or female) from the United States to report from the line of battle and the first reporter ever to interview Queen Mary of England.
	Rinehart goes into the newly formed Glacier Park, covering 300 miles by horseback; she writes *Through Glacier Park* about her experiences.
1916	Mary Roberts Rinehart and her family ride through Glacier Park on horseback, raft the Flathead River, and ride through the Cascades, which provided material for her book *Tenting Tonight*.
	Elinore Pruitt Stewart takes her family on camping trips in Wyoming.
	Dora Keen marries George Handy.
	Mary Jobe opens Camp Mystic for girls and invites noted explorers to share their adventures with her campers.
	The first woman is elected to the U.S. House of Representatives.
1917	*The first birth control clinic opens in the United States.*
	The United States enters World War I.
1917–1918	Elinore Pruitt Stewart raises a war garden, sells war bonds, does Red Cross work, and takes on extra ranch duties when the family's ranch hand leaves for the war. President Woodrow Wilson later praises her efforts.

Grace Gallatin Seton directs a women's motor unit that provides relief work in France; she is decorated by the French government for her work.

1918   *Canadian women receive the right to vote.*

1918–1919   Marion Randall Parsons, working for the Red Cross in France, is placed in charge of providing relief for refugees; she is decorated by the French government for her efforts.

1919   *The League of Women Voters is founded.*

1920s

1920   *The Nineteenth Amendment to the U.S. Constitution passes and women receive the right to vote.*

1920s   Grace Gallatin Seton travels to Egypt, China, and India and writes *A Woman Tenderfoot in Egypt, Chinese Lanterns,* and "*Yes, Lady Saheb*" about her travels.

1923   Mary Roberts Rinehart's third outdoor adventure book, *The Out Trail*, is published.

1924   Mary Jobe marries Carl Akeley.

             A woman is elected governor of Wyoming, the first woman to hold the office of governor in the United States.

1925   The Society of Woman Geographers is founded; Grace Gallatin Seton is one of eight original members. Annie Peck joins the organization three years later.

1926   Mary Jobe Akeley accompanies her husband to Africa; when he dies there she continues his work, becoming an adviser to the African Hall at the American Museum of Natural History in New York.

1928   *Women compete in the Olympics for the first time.*

1930s

1930s   Grace Gallatin Seton travels in South America and Southeast Asia, writing *Magic Waters* and *Poison Arrows*.

1932   Annie Peck, at age eighty-one, climbs 5,366-foot Mount Madison in New Hampshire.

Miriam Underhill leads an all-woman team to the summit of the Matterhorn, the first ascent of the mountain without men.

Amelia Earhart is the first woman in history to fly solo across the Atlantic Ocean.

The first woman is elected to the U.S. Senate.

1933   Dora Keen Handy and George Handy are divorced.

Elinore Pruitt Stewart dies at age fifty-seven from a blood clot in the brain.

Frances Perkins becomes U.S. Secretary of Labor, the first woman appointed to the president's cabinet.

1933–1938   Grace Gallatin Seton serves as chair of letters of the National Council of Women and organizes the Conclave of Women Writers and the Biblioteca Femina.

1935   Grace Gallatin Seton and Ernest Thompson Seton are divorced.

Annie Peck dies at the age of eighty-four after cancelling a world tour.

1935–1936   Mary Jobe Akeley tours parts of Africa, surveying wildlife and collecting information about traditional culture.

1940s

1940s   Marion Randall Parsons's paintings are exhibited in California; a book of her paintings is published in 1952.

1942	*Women are admitted for the first time to the International Brotherhood of Boilermakers, Iron Shipbuilders and Helpers.*
1945	*Women in France receive the right to vote.*
1948	*A woman becomes a jet pilot for the first time.*
1949	*A woman serves as U.S. ambassador for the first time.*

1950s

1950s	Dora Keen travels extensively.
1953	Marion Randall Parsons dies at age seventy-four.
1956	*The first female pilot flies for a commercial airline.*
1958	Mary Roberts Rinehart dies at age eighty-two.
1959	Grace Gallatin Seton dies at age eighty-seven.

1960s

1961	*The first U.S. Presidential Commission on the Status of Women is established.*
1962	Dora Keen embarks on a world tour and dies en route, in 1963, at age ninety-one.
	Rachel Carson writes Silent Spring, *launching the environmental movement.*
1963	*Betty Friedan writes* The Feminine Mystique, *launching the women's movement.*
1966	Mary Jobe Akeley dies at age seventy-eight.
	The National Organization for Women (NOW) is founded.

1970s

1971   Ms. *magazine begins publication.*

1974   *Girls are admitted to Little League.*

1975   *Junko Tabei, climbing with a female Japanese team, is the first woman to reach the summit of Mount Everest.*

1976   *A woman coanchors a daily network news program for the first time.*

1978   *Arlene Blum leads the first American all-woman team to Annapurna, a peak in the Himalayas.*

             Beverly Johnson is the first woman to climb El Capitan in Yosemite.

NOTES

x   Dora Keen and Mary Jobe: Because Dora Keen and Mary Jobe gained prominence as single women, I have used their birth names rather than their married names for chapter titles and other references.

xii   Women not included: Three notable women of this era have not been included here. Because I focused on women from the Americas who sought adventure in the Americas, I left out the British Isabella L. Bird, whose trip on horseback in Colorado in the 1870s was truly phenomenal. She wrote of this trip in *A Lady's Life in the Rocky Mountains.* I also omitted Fanny Bullock Workman, mentioned in the chapter about Annie Peck, because she made her name in the Himalayas rather than in the Western Hemisphere.

The story of Mina Benson Hubbard, a Canadian who canoed through Labrador in 1905, is well documented in *Great Heart: The History of a Labrador Adventure.* Although Mina was indeed courageous, she undertook the journey solely to prove that her husband (who had died on the same trip two years before) had been right in his assessment that the trip could be done. She did not have a thirst for adventure that compelled her to set out on other trips thereafter.

xii   Economic and employment data: Banner 1984, 8.

Chapter 1: Martha Whitman

1   "For the first time I realized": Whitman 1877, 134.

3   "It was, to put it mildly": Waterman and Waterman 1989, 119.

3   "I desire to let [women] know" and other quotes describing her camping trips: Whitman 1878.

6   Wool clothing: Wool remained the fabric of choice for camping for over a hundred years until synthetic fibers came into general use in the 1980s.

6   Allowing women to join: The Appalachian Mountain Club had voted to accept women members at its second meeting, and although men occupied the leadership roles there were often more women than men on trips. According to the Watermans (1989, 191), the decision to allow women to join contributed to the club's growth into a major outdoor organization in the Northeast.

7   Whitman's companion: Whitman's companion may have been Augustus Scott, who was, over time, a teacher, principal, and attorney in Lexington. He and Whitman were the only AMC members from Lexington in

1877 and both were active in the Lexington Field and Garden Club. Together they explored the Pemigewasset Wilderness and Twin Mountain Range, and Whitman is described as one of Scott's "efficient lieutenants" by Marion Pychowska. Scott became president of the AMC the year of Whitman's death.

8   "Merry and enthusiastic": Scott 1883, 116.

8   "Evidently very independent": Letter from Marion Pychowska to Isabella Stone on September 3, 1882, in Rowan and Rowan 1995, 102.

8   "In the physical condition of women": *Boston Medical and Surgical Journal* 1855, 292–293. Although seventeen medical schools for women were opened in the nineteenth century, opposition to women doctors was still strong. After a fierce internal battle, the Massachusetts Medical Society did vote to allow women members in 1884, but the organization's journal editorialized strongly against the move. Most women's schools had ceased operations by 1903, and women found it increasingly difficult to gain admittance to coeducational programs (Miller 1994, 602–603).

8   Medical school thesis: Whitman's thesis was about the reliability of medical expert testimony.

9   Excerpt: Whitman 1878, 131–137.

CHAPTER 2: E. PAULINE JOHNSON

17   "We ran our first rapids": Johnson 1891, 51.

19   The trip with Joe: Johnson 1892b, 45–48.

19   "Thrilling was the effect" and "rarely does an audience": Frank Yeigh in "An Appreciation," *Everywoman's World,* February 1918 quoted in Foster 1931, 39.

20   "August is laughing across the sky": From "The Song My Paddle Sings" in Van Steen 1965, 97–99.

21   Top woman paddler: Van Steen 1965, 13.

21   Birch canoe: Seton was using poetic license; the *Wildcat* was wood and canvas.

22   "Never let anyone call me a white woman": Recounted by naturalist Ernest Thompson Seton in his introduction to *The Shagganappi.*

23   "Whenever she felt bruised": Van Steen 1965, 12–13.

23   "The defeat of love": Mair 1913, 281.

24   Paddling in Vancouver: Keller 1981, 238.

24   "When we are born": *Vancouver Province,* March 5, 1913, in Foster 1931, 145.

25   "In spite of her English mother": L. W. Makovski in *Vancouver Province,* in Foster 1931, 151–152.

25   Excerpt: Johnson 1891, 48–52.

CHAPTER 3: ANNIE SMITH PECK

37 "The chief joy": Peck 1901, 695.

38 "You'll be twenty-seven": Reported in Niles 1937, 43.

38 "On beholding:" Peck 1911, ix.

39 "The exercise was delightful": Peck 1911, ix.

39 "When I cannot get what I want": Letter to Isabel Howland, October 9, 1892, Howland Papers, Smith College Archives.

39 "If you are determined to commit suicide": Reported in Greenwood 1987, 46.

40 "Men, we all know": Peck 1901, 698–699.

40 "Mountain climbing, I thought": Peck 1911, x.

41 "My next thought" and "from the earliest years": Peck 1911, x–xi.

41 "Never before had I felt so helpless": Peck 1906a, 101.

41 "Especially should those who desire": Membership solicitation, Peck Papers, Smith College Archives.

45 "Surely I hope again to climb": Peck 1911, xii.

45 Peck's age: Blair Niles (1937, 42), a friend of Peck's at the Society of Woman Geographers, wrote that at age eighty Peck confided, "It always seemed best not to tell my age but now that I am eighty my friends say that it can't do any harm to tell."

45 "If, as seems probable": Peck 1909a, 187.

46 "I am only following": Earhart on book jacket of *Flying over South America* (Peck 1932).

46 "Where my trunk is": Peck 1911, 202.

47 Excerpt: Peck 1909b, 43, 70–71.

CHAPTER 4: DORA KEEN

55 "A new feeling of confidence": Keen 1912a, 768.

55 "Worthy of the hardiest mountaineer": Keen 1912a, 765. Other quotes about the first expedition to Mount Blackburn are from Keen 1912a unless otherwise noted.

56 "For the wonderful views": Keen 1911, 643.

58 "No one ropes": The sourdoughs who climbed McKinley used poleaxes and double-bit axes to cut steps in the ice but did not even take a rope.

60 "A new spirit": Keen 1912b, 339.

61 Mount Saint Elias: It was thought that Mount Saint Elias was the only high Alaskan peak that had been climbed. Keen had heard that four sourdoughs claimed to have climbed Mount McKinley in 1910, but McKinley had turned back several well-planned expeditions, so it seemed impossible that

local miners with no mountaineering experience had gained the highly sought summit. When the Karstens-Stuck party climbed the South Peak (the true, higher peak) in 1913, they saw the flagpole the sourdoughs had placed on the North Peak, and the miners were vindicated. The sourdoughs, in fact, had pioneered the quick-ascent strategy in mountaineering—they had gone from their highest camp at 10,900 feet to the 19,450-foot summit and returned to the camp in one day. Keen used this same strategy on Mount Blackburn.

61   "With some mistrust": Keen 1913, 80. Other quotes about this trip are also from Keen 1913.

62   Trip to Yukon River: Aldeman 1926, 312.

63   "I believe more and more": Keen 1915b, 52.

63   "Where others filled their winters": *New York World,* August 6, 1916.

64   "All over the world": Bryn Mawr Alumnae Survey 1961.

64   "Just filled with old people": Freeman 1963, 540.

64   "I thirst for adventure" and climbing details: O'Donnell 1996, 32–34. Freeman 1963, 540, also reports that Keen included this comment in a letter.

64   Excerpt: Keen 1913, 88–101.

78   "16,140-foot subarctic peak": The peak is actually 16,380 feet high.

CHAPTER 5: GRACE GALLATIN SETON

81   "I have felt the charm": Seton 1905, 358–361.

82   Description of Ernest Seton: *Toronto Globe* February 11, 1893, quoted in Keller 1984, 143–144.

82   Ernest Thompson Seton: Ernest was born Ernest Evan Thompson but took on Seton, a supposed family surname, in 1883. Over the years he used Thompson, Seton-Thompson, and Thompson Seton. Although he called himself Thompson when he met Grace and she became Mrs. Ernest Thompson, in 1901 he legally changed his name to Ernest Thompson Seton, the name used here. Grace also used several professional names. Her first book, in 1900, came out under the name Grace Gallatin Thompson Seton. In 1907 she used Grace Gallatin Seton, and in later books she used Grace Thompson Seton.

82   A ranch in North Dakota: The Setons stayed at the Eaton Ranch, run by Howard Eaton and his brothers. Howard later guided Mary Roberts Rinehart through Glacier Park.

82   Creature comforts: G. Seton 1907, 74–75.

82   "As a camper": E. Seton 1940, 439.

82   Took over the management of Ernest's books: Keller 1984, 147.

83   "Always regulate your fears": G. Seton 1905, 111.

83 Laying the foundation for a separate career: Keller 1984, 147.

85 "Gave all her time to reform work" and other quotes: Kinkaid 1912, 153. The curious reader wonders whether Seton made the comment about being so proud of inventing new dishes and designing gowns. If so, she was well versed in addressing the audience at hand; when writing for *Tenderfoot* readers she wrote proudly of how she learned to handle her horse and control her fears.

85 "Although Mrs. Seton's bearing": Lafferty 1940.

87 Seton believed in women's rights: Seton described herself as "one of those people who were born believing in suffrage" (Feinberg 1980, 639).

88 Excerpt: G. Seton 1905, 19–27, 31–40, 88–91, 195–201, 357–361.

CHAPTER 6: ELINORE PRUITT STEWART

99 "I wanted to just knock about": Stewart 1914, 188. Note references are to Stewart's letters as collected in *Letters of a Woman Homesteader* rather than their appearance in *Atlantic Monthly*.

100 The Chickasaw Nation: The Chickasaw is a Muskogean-speaking tribe that once lived in what is now northern Mississippi and part of Tennessee. The Chickasaw ceded their land to the United States in an 1832 treaty and purchased land in Oklahoma Territory from the Choctaw in early 1837. The following summer many tribal members moved to the new land. Stewart's grandmother, who was born in 1826, arrived in the treaty area sometime before 1840, perhaps with the 1837 wave.

100 Stewart's father: Josephine Courtney married a Mr. Pruitt (first name unknown) and had one child, Elinore; when he died while serving in the military Josephine married his brother, Thomas, and had eight more children.

100 "Well, we had no money": Stewart 1914, 16.

101 "The rattle and the bang" and "nothing but the mountains": Stewart 1914, 226, 189.

101 Placed an ad: Elinore wrote in *Homesteader* that she placed the ad, but her biographer's research showed that it was Stewart who did so. George (1992, 11) suggests the editing of events occurred because Elinore may have wanted to present herself as taking charge of her future rather than simply responding to an ad.

101 Moving to Wyoming: Whereas Grace Gallatin Seton worked hard to gain the right to vote, Stewart automatically qualified when she moved to Wyoming. Wyoming's constitution, which went into effect when it joined the Union in 1890, was the first to grant women the right to vote.

101 Details of filing: Smith 1991, 165–167.

101 "It was too beautiful a night to sleep": Stewart 1914, 11.

102 "I had not thought" and other quotes about getting married: Stewart 1914, 134, 185, 188. Indeed, the shortness of the engagement and the fact that Elinore filed for land adjacent to Clyde's suggest that she was a bit disingenuous about being a single woman homesteader. She did not build a separate home and live in it, as the law required; instead, she and Clyde simply extended his house onto her property.

102 "Had enough cut" and "almost as much sense": Stewart 1914, 17.

103 "We got away": Stewart, 1914, 18.

103 "Interesting happenings": Sedgwick 1945, 197 quoted in George 1992, 18.

103 "There is no assumption of finished style": *Book Review Digest* 1916, 440.

104 The persona of the Woman Homesteader: George (1992, *passim*, including 128, 203, 208–209) puts forth and develops the idea of this persona.

104 "To me, homesteading is the solution": Stewart 1914, 215.

104 Book payment: Stewart also received royalty checks twice a year.

105 Run out of paper: George 1992, 42.

105 "A readable little book" and other reviews: *Book Review Digest* 1915, 509, and 1916, 440.

105 "Dawn in the mountains": Stewart 1915, 97–98.

106 Elinore's camping trips in 1916: Mary Roberts Rinehart took her own family camping the same year. The Rineharts rode on horseback through Glacier Park, boated the Flathead River, and rode horses through the Cascades.

106 Elinore's changing style: George 1992, 207.

106 Elinore as a role model: Smith (1991, 176–177) wrote that it is doubtful that poor women took up homesteading as a result of reading *A Woman Homesteader* because Stewart's audience consisted of urban readers from the middle and upper classes. Stewart, a strong and independent woman, may still have served as a role model in a wider sense.

106 "I just love people": Quoted in George 1992, 197.

107 Life as an adventure: George 1992, 209.

107 Excerpt: Stewart 1914, 23–44.

CHAPTER 7: MARY ROBERTS RINEHART

119 "If you are normal and philosophical": Rinehart 1916, 3–4.

120 Rinehart's trip to the front: Rinehart also interviewed King Albert of Belgium and Queen Mary of England, notable achievements for a reporter from the United States. When signing the queen's register, Mary debated whether to use her married name, Mrs. Stanley Rinehart, or her professional name, Mary Roberts Rinehart. She opted for the latter.

120 "Improper and immodest" and "bold": Rinehart 1948, 34.

120 "A queer jumble": Rinehart 1948, 33.

120 Economically helpless: In her autobiography (Rinehart 1948, 21), Rinehart comments on the difficulties of being a young woman in the 1880s.

121 "The household drudge I was": Unpublished autobiographical material in Cohn 1980, 27.

121 Tish as Rinehart's alter ego: This information comes from one of Rinehart's sons (Welter 1980, 578 in Sicherman and Green). In her autobiography, Rinehart relates an amusing incident that occurred when she and a woman friend were traveling in the Mexican backcountry. A man approached her and asked if she had ever read stories about a woman named "Tish." "Yes," she answered. "Why?" "Well, somehow today you remind me of her," he answered (Rinehart 1948, 247).

122 "I've felt for a long time" and "I'm so glad": Rinehart 1931, Section 1, 263, 266.

122 "No feminist" and "those women": Rinehart 1948, 320, 322.

122 "Four times as much": Rinehart, Up and Down with the Drama, Saturday Evening Post, July 6, 1912, cited in Cohn 1980, 40.

124 "Hoping to spend": Letter to Grace Gallatin Seton, April 7, 1933.

124 "So perhaps I have done some good": Rinehart 1948, 522.

125 Excerpt: Rinehart 1918, 64–70, 81–86, 127–128, 130–136.

CHAPTER 8: MARY JOBE

135 Pronunciation of Jobe: Jobe rhymes with "robe."

135 "It began at Winnipeg in June": Jobe 1915a, 813.

136 "Carefully reared" and "I had always wanted to be a boy": Akeley 1936, 166.

136 Details about Jobe's Canadian expeditions: Smith 1989, 80–104.

137 "Obviously, here was a chance": Jobe 1915a, 813.

137 "There are many places": Jobe 1915a, 814.

139 Unsuccessful in gaining the summit: Mount Sir Alexander was not climbed until 1928, when a party of three—including a woman—reached the summit.

139 "At no time": Jobe 1918b, 88–89.

140 "Aristocratic" and "even in baggy bloomers": Kimball 1978, 1.

140 "Plucky brunette": New York Times 1966, 31.

140 Delia Akeley and the divorce: Olds 1985, 113.

141 "The whole circle of the heavens": Akeley 1929, 66.

142 "It is almost impossible" and "we both had felt": Akeley 1929, 189.

142 "Today the wild animals of Africa": *New York Times* 1966, 31.

142 "Journey of rediscovery": McCay 1980, 9.

143 "Whose lot throughout the years": Akeley 1950, 184.

143 Excerpt: Jobe 1915a, 817–825.

145 Glacial features: A glacier creates a *moraine* by bringing forward rocks imbedded in the ice and depositing them in a ridge at the front edge (*terminal moraine*) or along its sides (*lateral moraine*). An *arête* is a knife-edged ridge such as one created when two glacial basins become enlarged so that only a thin, sharp ridge remains between them. A *serac* is the pileup of ice that forms when two or more glaciers merge. A *crevasse* is a deep, vertical fissure in the ice.

CHAPTER 9: MARION RANDALL PARSONS

153 "We reached the rocks at last": Parsons 1910a, 176.

154 "For a little while" and "these things": Randall 1905, 99.

154 "The aristocrat of good-fellowship": Randall 1905, 97.

154 "Their vigor and endurance": Sexton 1902, 92.

155 "Confusion was no word" and "the arrangement proved unexpectedly happy": Parsons 1916, 33.

155 "A task to which she brought devotion": Badè 1917, viii.

156 "We women who 'knapsack'": Parsons 1915, 422.

156 "Our personal outfits": Parsons 1915, 421–422, 424.

157 "But there is perhaps": Parsons 1912, 179.

158 "I had dreamed" and other quotes about climbing Mount Robson: Parsons 1919, 36.

158 Parsons in France: Grace Gallatin Seton also worked in France at this time, and the curious reader wonders if the two women ever met.

158 "It was like old times": Parsons 1921, 134.

158 The Alps: Parsons 1926, 289–296.

159 "We still tread": Parsons 1930, 9+.

160 Excerpt: Parsons 1910a, 172–179.

BIBLIOGRAPHY

PREFACE

Banner, Lois W. 1984. *Women in Modern America: A Brief History.* Orlando: Harcourt Brace College Publishers, Harcourt Brace Jovanovich.

CHAPTER 1: MARTHA WHITMAN

[Editorial] "Females as Physicians." 1855. *Boston Medical and Surgical Journal* 53 (4): 292–294.

Hudson, Charles. 1913. *History of the Town of Lexington* 1: History, 2: Genealogies. Boston: Houghton Mifflin.

Kilgore, Kathleen. 1991. *Transformations: A History of Boston University.* Boston: Boston University.

Miller, Joseph M. 1994. Vignette of Medical History: The First Women's Medical School. *Maryland Medical Journal* 43 (July): 601–603.

Rowan, Peter, and June Hammond Rowan, eds. 1995. *Mountain Summers.* Gorham, N.H.: Gulfside.

Scott, Augustus E. 1883. The Twin Mt. Range. *Appalachia* 3 (April): 107–121.

Waterman, Laura, and Guy Waterman. 1989. *Forest and Crag: A History of Hiking, Trail Blazing, and Adventure in the Northeast Mountains.* Boston: Appalachian Mountain Club.

Whitman, Martha F. 1877. A Climb Through Tuckerman's Ravine. *Appalachia* 1 (June): 131–137.

———. 1878. Camp Life for Ladies. *Appalachia* 2 (June): 44–48.

CHAPTER 2: E. PAULINE JOHNSON

Foster, Anne (Mrs. W. Garland Foster). 1931. *The Mohawk Princess: Being Some Account of the Life of Tekahion-wake (E. Pauline Johnson).* Vancouver: Lions' Gate.

Johnson, E. Pauline. 1891. Ripples and Paddle Splashes: A Canoe Story. *Outing* 19 (October): 48–52.

———. 1892a. Indian Medicine Men and Their Magic. *Dominion Illustrated* (April).

———. 1892b. A Week in the "Wild Cat." *Outing* 23 (October): 45–48.

———. 1893a. A Red Girl's Reasoning. *Dominion Illustrated* (February).

———. 1893b. Iroquois of Grand River. *Harper's Weekly* 38 (June 23).

———. 1895. *The White Wampum.* London: Bodley Head.

———. 1898. Organization of Iroquois. *Canada* 1.

———. 1903. *Canadian Born.* Toronto: Morang.

———. 1911. *Legends of Vancouver.* Toronto: Sunset. Reprint, McClelland, Stewart, 1912.

———. 1912. *Flint and Feather.* Toronto: Musson.

———. 1913a. *The Moccasin Maker.* Toronto: Briggs.

———. 1913b. *The Shagganappi.* Toronto: Briggs.

Keller, Betty. 1981. *Pauline: A Biography of Pauline Johnson.* Vancouver: Douglas and McIntyre.

Mackay, Isabel E. 1913. Pauline Johnson: A Reminiscence. *Canada Magazine* 41 (July): 273–279.

Mair, Charles. 1913. Pauline Johnson: An Appreciation. *Canada Magazine* 41 (July): 281–283.

McRaye, Walter. 1947. *Pauline Johnson and Her Friends.* Toronto: Ryerson.

Van Steen, Marcus. 1965. *Pauline Johnson: Her Life and Work.* Toronto: Musson.

CHAPTER 3: ANNIE SMITH PECK

Briggs, Berta. 1970. Annie Smith Peck. In *Notable American Women 1807–1950: A Biographical Dictionary,* vol. 3, Edward T. James, Janet Wilson James, and Paul S. Boyer, eds. Cambridge: Harvard University Press.

Greenwood, Sallie. 1987. A Frame of Reference: Historical Perspective. *Climbing* 103 (August): 44–46.

Howland Papers, Smith College Archives, Northampton, Mass.

Men and Women of the Outdoor World. 1903. *Outing* 42 (August): 623–624.

Niles, Blair. 1937. *Peruvian Pageant.* New York: Bobbs-Merrill.

Olds, Elisabeth Fagg. 1985. *Women of the Four Winds: The Adventures of Four of America's First Women Explorers.* Boston: Houghton Mifflin.

Peck, Annie S. 1901. Practical Mountain Climbing. *Outing* 28 (September): 695–700.

———. 1906a. Climbing Mount Sorata. *Appalachia* 11 (May): 95–110.

———. 1906b. A Woman in the Andes. *Harper's Monthly* 64 (December): 3–14.

———. 1909a. The First Ascent of Mount Huascaran. *Harper's Monthly* 68 (January): 173–187.

———. 1909b. The Most Dramatic Event in My Life. *Delineator* 74 (July): 43, 70–71.

———. 1910. Miss Peck Replies to Mrs. Workman. *Scientific American* 102 (February 26): 183.

———. 1911. *A Search for the Apex of America: High Mountain Climbing in Peru and Bolivia, Including the Conquest of Huascaran, with Some Observations on the Country and People Below.* New York: Dodd, Mead.

Peck Papers, Smith College Archives, Northampton, Mass.

Peck Papers, Society of Woman Geographers Archives, Washington, D.C.

Waterman, Laura, and Guy Waterman. 1981. The Indomitable Annie Smith Peck: Conqueror of Mountains. *New England Outdoors* (June): 15–17, 46.

Workman, Fanny Bullock. 1910. Miss Peck and Mrs. Workman. *Scientific American* 102 (February 12): 143.

CHAPTER 4: DORA KEEN

Aldeman, Joseph. 1926. *Famous Women.* New York: Ellis M. Lonow.

Alpina. 1915. *Appalachia* 13 (December): 391–393.

Freeman, William W. K. 1963. In Memoriam: Dora Keen Handy. *Appalachia* 29 (June): 539–540.

Keen, Dora. 1911. A Woman's Climbs in the High Alps. *National Geographic* 22 (July): 642–675.

———. 1912a. Arctic Mountaineering by a Woman: Mount Blackburn. *Scribner's* 52 (July): 764–780.

———. 1912b. Mountain Climbing in Alaska: The First Expedition to Mount Blackburn. *Appalachia* 12 (April): 327–339.

———. 1913. First up Mt. Blackburn. *World's Work* 27 (November): 80–101.

———. 1915a. Exploring the Harvard Glacier. *Harper's Monthly* 132 (December): 113–125.

———. 1915b. News from the Class. *Bryn Mawr Alumnae Quarterly* (April): 52.

———. 1961. Bryn Mawr Alumnae Survey, Keen Papers, Bryn Mawr College Archives, Bryn Mawr, Pa.

Leonard, John William, ed. 1914. *Woman's Who's Who of America, 1914–1915.* New York: American Commonwealth.

New York World. 1916. The Romance of the Seventh Man (August 6).

O'Donnell, Neil. 1996. Against All Odds: Dora Keen's Revolutionary First Ascent of Mt. Blackburn. *Rock & Ice* 72 (March–April): 32–34.

CHAPTER 5: GRACE GALLATIN SETON

Buckler, Helen, Mary F. Fielder, and Martha F. Allen. 1961. *Wo-He-Lo: The Story of Camp Fire Girls.* New York: Holt, Rinehart and Winston.

Feinberg, Joan. 1980. Grace Gallatin Seton. In *Notable American Women, the Modern Period,* Barbara Sicherman and Carol Hurd Green, eds. Cambridge: Harvard University Press.

Keller, Betty. 1984. *Black Wolf: The Life of Ernest Thompson Seton.* Vancouver: Douglas and McIntyre.

Kinkaid, Mary Holland. 1912. The Feminine Charms of the Woman Militant. *Good Housekeeping* 54 (February): 153.

Lafferty, Margaret C. 1940. Grace Thompson Seton Is Author of "Poison Arrows." *Times-Union* (Jacksonville, Florida, April 21).

Seton, Ernest Thompson. 1940. *The Trail of an Artist-Naturalist: The Autobiography of Ernest Thompson Seton.* New York: Charles Scribner's Sons.

Seton, Grace Gallatin. 1905. *A Woman Tenderfoot.* New York: Doubleday, Page. Originally published as *A Woman Tenderfoot in the Rockies.* London: David Nutt, 1900.

———. 1907. *Nimrod's Wife.* London: Archibald, Constable.

———. 1923. *A Woman Tenderfoot in Egypt.* New York: Dodd, Mead.

———. 1924. *Chinese Lanterns.* New York: Dodd, Mead.

———. 1925. *"Yes, Lady Saheb": A Woman's Adventurings with Mysterious India.* New York: Harper and Brothers.

———. 1933. *Magic Waters.* New York: E. P. Dutton. Originally published as *Log of the "Look-See."* London: Hurst and Blackett, 1932.

———. 1938. *Poison Arrows.* New York: House of Field.

———. 1947. *The Singing Traveler.* Boston: Christopher.

Seton, Grace [Gallatin] Thompson. 1965. *The National Cyclopaedia of American Biography.* 47. New York: James T. White.

Seton Papers, Sophia Smith Collection, Smith College Archives, Northampton, Mass.

CHAPTER 6: ELINORE PRUITT STEWART

George, Suzanne K. 1992. *The Adventures of a Woman Homesteader.* Lincoln: University of Nebraska Press.

Book Review Digest. 1915. Stewart, Mrs. Elinore (Pruitt). 10: 509.

Book Review Digest. 1916. Stewart, Mrs. Elinore (Pruitt). 11: 440.

Smith, Sherry L. 1991. Single Women Homesteaders: The Perplexing Case of Elinore Pruitt Stewart. *Western Historical Quarterly* 22 (May): 163–183.

Stewart, Elinore Pruitt. 1914, 1988. *Letters of a Woman Homesteader.* Boston: Houghton Mifflin Company. (First published in *Atlantic Monthly* October 1913 through April 1914.)

———. 1915. *Letters on an Elk Hunt.* Boston: Houghton Mifflin Company. Reprint, Lincoln: University of Nebraska Press, 1979. (First published in *Atlantic Monthly* February 1914 through May 1915.)

CHAPTER 7: MARY ROBERTS RINEHART

Cohn, Jan. 1980. *Improbable Fiction: The Life of Mary Roberts Rinehart.* Pittsburgh: University of Pittsburgh Press.

Moses, Montrose J. 1917. Mary Roberts Rinehart—Author, Wife, and Mother. *Good Housekeeping* 64 (April): 30–31, 97–99.

Rinehart, Mary Roberts. 1916. *Through Glacier Park: Seeing America First with Howard Eaton.* Boston: Houghton Mifflin.

———. 1917. The Altar of Freedom. *Saturday Evening Post* (April 21).

———. 1918, 1928. *Tenting Tonight: A Chronicle of Sport and Adventure in Glacier Park and the Cascade Mountains.* New York: Doubleday, Doran.

———. 1923. *The Out Trail.* New York: George H. Doran.

———. 1931. *The Book of Tish.* New York: Farrer and Rinehart.

———. 1933. Letter to Grace Gallatin Seton, April 7, 1933. Seton Papers, Sophia Smith Collection, Smith College Archives, Northampton, Mass.

———. 1931, 1948. *My Story.* New York: Rinehart.

Welter, Barbara. 1980. Mary Roberts Rinehart. In *Notable American Women, the Modern Period,* Barbara Sicherman and Carol Hurd Green, eds. Cambridge: Harvard University Press.

CHAPTER 8: MARY JOBE

Akeley, Carl, and Mary L. Jobe Akeley. 1931. *Adventures in the African Jungle.* New York: Junior Literary Guild.

———. 1932. *Lions, Gorillas and Their Neighbors.* New York: Dodd, Mead.

Akeley, Mary L. Jobe. 1928. Carl Akeley's Last Journey. *World's Work* 56 (July): 250–259.

———. 1929. *Carl Akeley's Africa.* New York: Dodd, Mead.

———. 1936. *The Restless Jungle.* New York: Robert M. McBride.

———. 1940. *The Wilderness Lives Again: Carl Akeley and the Great Adventure.* New York: Dodd, Mead.

———. 1950. *Congo Eden.* New York: Dodd, Mead.

———. 1954. Alumnae Association Update Questionnaire (February 12). Archival material at Mariam Coffin Canaday Library, Bryn Mawr College, Bryn Mawr, Pa.

Jobe, Mary L. 1915a. My Quest in the Canadian Rockies. *Harper's* 130 (May): 813–825.

———. 1915b. The Expedition to "Mt. Kitchi": A New Peak in the Canadian Rockies. *Canadian Alpine Journal* 6: 188–200.

———. 1916. Mt. Alexander Mackenzie. *Canadian Alpine Journal* 7: 82–99.

———. 1918a. A Winter Journey Through the Northern Canadian Rockies: From Mt. Robson to Mt. Sir Alexander. *Appalachia* 14 (June): 223–233.

———. 1918b. A Winter Journey to Mt. Sir Alexander and the Wapiti. *Canadian Alpine Journal* 9: 79–89.

Kimball, Carol W. 1978. Camp Mystic in the Good Old Summertime. *Historical Footnotes, Bulletin of the Stonington Historical Society* 15 (February): 1–11.

McCay, Mary. 1980. Mary Lee Jobe Akeley. In *Notable American Women, the Modern Period*, Barbara Sicherman and Carol Hurd Green, eds. Cambridge: Harvard University Press.

New York Times. 1966. Obituary: Mary J. Akeley. July 22: 31.

Olds, Elizabeth Fagg. 1985. *Women of the Four Winds*. Boston: Houghton Mifflin.

Smith, Cyndi. 1989. *Off the Beaten Track: Women Adventurers and Mountaineers in Western Canada*. Jasper: Coyote.

CHAPTER 9: MARION RANDALL PARSONS

Appalachian Mountain Club. 1915. Alpina: Elections to the American Alpine Club. *Appalachia* 13 (December): 392–393.

Badè, William Frederic. 1917. Preface. In *Travels in Alaska* by John Muir. Boston: Houghton Mifflin.

Gilliam, Ann, ed. 1979. *Voices for the Earth*. San Francisco: Sierra Club Books.

Lehmann, B. H. 1953. Marion Randall Parsons. *Sierra Club Bulletin* 38: 35–39.

Parsons, Marion Randall. 1909. With the Sierra Club in the Kern Cañon. *Sierra Club Bulletin* 7 (January): 23–32.

———. 1910a. On Mt. St. Helens with the Mazamas. *Sierra Club Bulletin* 7 (January): 170–179.

———. 1910b. The Sierra Club. *Annals of the American Academy of Political and Social Science* 35 (March): 420–425.

———. 1912. The Mazama Club Outing to Glacier Peak. *Sierra Club Bulletin* 8 (January): 174–185.

———. 1915. A Woman's Tramping Trip Through Yosemite. *Overland Monthly* n.s. 66 (November): 421–427.

———. 1916. John Muir and the Alaska Book. In *Voices for the Earth*, Ann Gilliam, ed.

———. 1918. A Week Around Mount Robson. *Sierra Club Bulletin* 10 (January): 269–275.

———. 1919. Negotiating Mt. Robson. *Travel* (September) 33: 35–39.

———. 1921. The 1920 Outing: Headwaters of the San Joaquin and the Kings. *Sierra Club Bulletin* 11 (January): 134–143.

———. 1923. *A Daughter of the Dawn*. Boston: Little, Brown.

———. 1926. Spring in the Tyrol. *Sierra Club Bulletin* 12: 289–296.

———. 1930. The Twenty-Eighth Outing. *Sierra Club Bulletin* 15: 9+.

———. 1952. *Old California Houses: Portraits and Stories*. Berkeley: University of California Press.

Randall, Marion. 1905. Why Camp with a Crowd? In *Voices for the Earth*, Ann Gilliam, ed.

Sexton, Ella M. 1902. Camp Muir in the Tuolumne Meadows. In *Voices for the Earth*, by Ann Gilliam, ed.

APPENDIX: CHRONOLOGY
Grum, Bernard. 1991. *The Timetables of History.* New York: Simon and Schuster. 3rd ed.
Read, Phyllis, and Bernard Witlieb. 1992. *The Book of Women's Firsts.* New York: Random House.
Trager, James. 1994. *The Women's Chronology.* New York: Henry Holt.
Zilboorg, Caroline, ed. 1997. *Women's Firsts.* Detroit: Gale Research.

INDEX

Page references for photographs, illustrations, and maps appear in italic. References in Notes are marked with "n."

Abruzzi, Duke of the, 58, 61
Adams, Ansel and Virginia, 159
Akeley, Carl, 140–41, 176
Akeley, Delia (Denning), 140
Akeley, Mary Jobe. *See* Jobe, Mary
Albert I, King of Belgium, 186n
Alexander, Mount Sir, 137, 139, 143–51, 174, 187n
altitude record, held by women, 40, 41, 45, 173
American Alpine Club, 41, 45, 62, 157
American Museum of Natural History, 49, 140–41, 142, 176
American Red Cross, 158, 176
American Woman Suffrage Association, 170, 171
Appalachian Mountain Club
    establishment of, 6, 170, 182n
    members: Kora Keen, 64; Augustus Scott, 181n; Martha Whitman, 6, 8, 170
    women, allowed to join, 170, 181–182n

Biblioteca Femina, 87, 177
Bird, Isabella, 39, 170, 181n
Blackburn, Mount
    Keen's first attempt, 55–60, 174
    Keen's second attempt, *60,* 61–62, 64–79, 174, 184n

Blackwell, Elizabeth, 169
Bloomer, Amelia, 169
Blum, Arlene, 179
Boston University Medical School, 8, 171
Bourne, Lizzie, 7, 14
Brevoort, Meta, 39, 40
British Columbia, 136–40, 157, 173
Bruce, Mount, 157, 175
Bryn Mawr College, 63, 136, 172

Camp Fire Girls, 85, 174
camping
    equipment for, 156–57
    how to, 4–6
Camp Mystic, 140, 175
cancer, breast, 24, 124
Carson, Rachel, 178
Cascade Mountains, 123, 175
Cather, Willa, 174
Chickasaw Nation, 100, 185n
clothing, for women
    for hiking and mountaineering, 5, 39–40, 44, 49, 159
    knickerbockers, 39–40, 49
    outdoor, xiv
    pantalettes, 169
    for riding, *84, 89*–91
Cloudy Pass, 123, 131–33
Coney, Juliet, 101, 102, 103, 107
Connecticut Woman's Suffrage Association, 85
Coropuna, Mount, 46, 174
Crosby, Cornelia "Fly Rod," 5

divorce, xiv

doctors, women as, 8, 169, 170, 171, 182n

Earhart, Amelia, 46, 177
Eaton, Howard, 123, 184n
education, women's, xii, 63. *See also* Bryn Mawr College; Smith College
employment, of women. *See* occupations, for women
Everest, Mount, 179

Flathead River, 123, 125–31, 175
Fraser River, 137
Friedan, Betty, 178
Fuller, Fay, 39, 171

Gallatin, Albert, 81, 170
Gallatin, Clemenzia (Rhodes), 81–82, 170
Girl Scouts of America, 174
Glacier National Park, 119–20, 121, 123, 175
glaciers, terms describing, 188n
guides, hired by
　Jobe, Mary, 137, 139
　Keen, Dora, 57, 79
　Parsons, Marion Randall, 158
　Peck, Annie, 38–39, 43
　Rinehart, Mary Roberts, 123, 184

Handy, Dora Keen. *See* Keen, Dora
Handy, George
　on Harvard Glacier expedition, 63, 174
　on Mount Blackburn expedition, 61–62, 64–79
　marriage and divorce, 63, 175, 177
Harvard Glacier, 63, 174

hiking, by women, 3, 156. *See also* clothing, for women; mountaineers, women
Holmes, Julia Archibald, 39, 169
homesteading, advice regarding, 104
Huascaran, Mount, 43–45, 47–53, 173
Hubbard, Mina Benson, 181n

Illampu, Mount (Sorata), 41, 43, 173
Indian Territory (now Oklahoma), 100, 170, 185n

Jobe, Mary
　birth and early life, 136, 171, 172
　death, 143, 178
　as director of Camp Mystic, 140, 175
　marriage, 140, 176
　as mountaineer, 136–39, 143–51, 158, 174
　portrait, *134, 138*
　travels, 136–40, 141–43, 173, 174, 176, 177
　and other women in *Adventurous Women*, xi–xiv, 139, 155
　works, 142–43
Jobe, Richard and Sarah (Pittis), 136, 171
Johnson, Beverly, 179
Johnson, Emily (Howells) and George, 17–18, 169
Johnson, E. Pauline (Tekahionwake)
　birth and early life, 17–19, 169
　as a canoeist, 18–19, 20–21, 25–35
　death, 24–25, 174
　engagement, 23
　portrait, *16*
　as a recitalist, 20–23, 171

and other women in *Adventurous Women,* ix–x, xii–xiv
works: *Canadian Born,* 24; "Ripples and Paddle Plashes," 25–35, 172; *Shagganappi,* 21; *Song My Paddle Sings,* 20–21, 172; *White Wampum,* 22
Johnson, Martin and Osa, 140
Johnson, Smoke (Tecahionwake), 18

Keen, Corinna (Borden) and William, 63, 170
Keen, Dora
  birth, early life, and education, 63, 170, 172
  climbs: Matterhorn, 56, 173; Mont Blanc, 173; Mount Blackburn, 55–60, *60,* 61–62, 64–70, 174, 184n; others, 56, 63, 173
  death, 64, 178
  encouragement of women, 63
  Harvard Glacier expedition, 63, 174
  later life, 63–64, 88, 178
  marriage and divorce, 63, 175, 177
  portrait, *54, 57*
  as suffragist, 63
  and other women in *Adventurous Women,* x, xii-xiv, 139
Kennicott Glacier. *See* Blackburn, Mount
knickerbockers. *See* clothing, for women

League of Women Voters, 176
Lexington Botanical Club, 3–4, 6
Lyman Lake, 123, 131–33

Madison, Mount, 46, 177

Mary, Queen of England, 175, 186n
Matterhorn, climbed by
  Keen, Dora, 56, 173
  Peck, Annie, 38, 39–49, 172, 173
  Underhill, Miriam (first ascent without men), 177
  other women, 38–39
Mazamas, 155
McKinley, 79, 183–184n
medicine, women in, 8, 169, 170, 171, 182n
Mohawk Nation, 18
mountaineers, women
  in Europe and the United States, 38–39
  See also Keen, Dora; Jobe, Mary; Parsons, Marion Randall; Peck, Annie; Whitman, Martha
Muir, John, 154, 155, 174
Muir, Wanda, 154, 172
Muskoka Lake, 18

National American Woman Suffrage Association, 171
National Organization for Women, 178
National Woman Suffrage Association, 170, 171
New England Female Medical College, 169, 170
Niles, Blair, 183n
Nineteenth Amendment, 176

occupations, for women, xii–xiii, 120, 122
Orizaba, Mount, 40

Parsons, Edward Taylor, *152,* 154–55, 173, 174

Parsons, Marion Randall
   birth and early life, 171, 172
   climbs, 154–59, 160–67, 175
   death, 159, 178
   marriage, 154, 173
   and John Muir, 155, 174
   portrait, *152*
   as Sierra Club member, 154–55,
      157–59, 172, 174
   and other women in *Adventurous
      Women*, xii–xiv, 137, 155, 158,
      159
   works, 157, 159, 177
   World War I, work during, 158,
      176
Peck, Annie Smith
   altitude record, 40, 41, 45, 173
   birth, early years, and education,
      38, 169, 170, 171
   climbs: Cloud's Rest, 39; Mount
      Coropuna, 46, 174; Mount
      Huascaran, 43–45,
      47–53, 173; Mount Illampu
      (Sorata), 41, 43; Matterhorn, 38,
      39–40, 172;
      Mount Madison, 46, 177; Mount
      Orizaba, 40; Mount Shasta, 39;
      Popocatépetl, 40
   clothing, views about, 39–40
   death, 46, 177
   later life, 39–46
   portrait, *36*
   Society of Woman Geographers,
      member of, 46, 87, 176
   as suffragist, 46, 174
   tour of South America by air,
      46
   and other women in *Adventurous
      Women*, x, xii–xiv, 139
   works, 44, 46, 88

Peck, Ann Power (Smith) and
   George, 169
Phillips, Donald, 137, 139, 143–51,
   158
Popocatépetl, 40
professions, for women, xii–xiii, 120,
   122
Pruitt, Elinore. *See* Stewart, Elinore
   Pruitt Rupert
Pruitt, Josephine (Courtney), 100,
   170, 172, 185n
Pychowska, Marion, 8, 182n

Randall, Charles and Nancy
   (Garabrant), 171
Randall, Marion. *See* Parsons, Marion
   Randall
Rinehart, Mary Roberts
   alter ego (Tish Carberry), 121, 187
   birth and early years, 120, 170, 171
   career, 121, 124–25, 173
   death, 125, 178
   marriage, 120, 172
   portrait, *118*
   travels, 119–20, 123, 124, 175,
      186–187n
   views on: economic status of
      women, 120; feminism and ca-
      reers for women, 122
   and other women in *Adventurous
      Women*, xi–xiv, 186n
   works: 123, 125, 173, 175, 176
   World War I, work during, 120,
      175, 186–87n
Rinehart, Stanley, 120, 124, 172
Roberts, Cornelia (Guilleland) and
   Tom, 120, 170
Rupert, Harry, 100, 172

Saint Helens, Mount, 155, 160–67

Sanger, Margaret, 174
Scott, Augustus, 181–182n
Seneca Falls, 169
Seton, Ann (Anya), 83, 87
Seton, Ernest Thompson
    divorce, 87, 177
    friendship with E. Pauline Johnson,
        21, 182n
    marriage, 82, 172
    names, various, 184n
    work, 82–83, 94–96
Seton, Grace Gallatin
    advice, regarding: fear, 83, 93–95;
        fortitude, 95–97; riding astride,
        91–92; women in
        the outdoors, 88–93
    Biblioteca Femina, formation of,
        87, 177
    birth and early years, 81–82, 170
    Camp Fire Girls, formation of, 85,
        174
    clothing, design for riding, *84,*
        89–91
    death, 87, 178
    divorce, 87, 177
    marriage 82, 172
    name, married, 184n
    portrait, *80*
    Society of Woman Geographers,
        formation of, 87, 176
    as suffragist, x, 85–86, 174, 185n
    travel: in Canada, 83; in the United
        States, 82, 172; around the
        world, 86, 176, 177
    World War I, work during, 86, 176
    and other women in *Adventurous
        Women,* x, xii–xiv
    works: *Nimrod's Wife,* 83, 173; *A
        Woman Tenderfoot,* 82–83, 172;
        others, 86, 176, 177

Sierra Club, 154–55, 157, 158–59,
    172, 173, 174
Six Nations, 18
Smith College, 39
Snow Arch, 7, 9–11
Society of Women Geographers, 46,
    87, 176, 183n
Springate, Margaret, 137, 147,
    151
Stefansson, Vilhjalmur, 62, 140
Stewart, Clyde, 101, 102, 106, 173,
    186n
Stewart, Elinore Pruitt Rupert
    advice, regarding homesteading,
        104
    birth, 100, 170, 185n
    on camping trips, 105, 106, 107–17,
        175
    death, 107, 177
    early life, 100, 171, 172
    homesteading: in Indian Territory,
        100, 172; in Wyoming, 101, 102,
        173
    marriage, to Harry Rupert, 100,
        172–73
    marriage, to Clyde Stewart, 102,
        173, 186n
    persona, as Woman Homesteader,
        104
    portrait, *98*
    as role model, 186n
    vote, right to, 185n
    works: *Letters of a Woman Home-
        steader,* 103–5, 174, 186n; *Letters
        on an Elk Hunt,* 105, 175; other
        works, 106
    and other women in *Adventurous
        Women,* xi–xiv, 186n
    World War I, work during, 106,
        175

suffrage, for women
  in Canada, 176
  in France, 178
  organizations promoting, 85, 170, 171, 176
  "suffragette" used in print, 173
  in United States, Nineteenth Amendment, 176
  See also Keen, Dora; Peck, Annie; Seton, Grace Gallatin

Taugwalder, Rudolf, 44, 45, 48–53
teachers, women as
  See occupations, for women
  See also Whitman, Martha; Peck, Annie; Keen, Dora; Jobe, Mary
Tekahionwake
  Johnson, Smoke, 18
  See also Johnson, E. Pauline
Tuckerman Ravine, 9–15
Twin Mountain Range, 8, 182n

Underhill, Miriam, 177

Walker, Lucy, 38–39, 40, 170
Washington, Mount, *2,* 6–7, 9–15
Waterman, Guy and Laura, 3, 181n
White Mountains, 2, 3–4, 6–7, 9–15, 171
Whitman, Jason and Mary (Fairfield), 169
Whitman, Martha Fairfield
  advice to women hikers, 3–6

Appalachian Mountain Club, membership in, 6, 170
birth, 169
camping trips, 3–6, 8, 170, 171, 182n
death, 8, 171
Lexington Botanical Club, membership in, 3–4, 6
medical school, 8, 171, 182n
Washington, Mount, ascent of, 6–7, 9–15, 170
and other women in *Adventurous Women,* ix, xii–xiv
Workman, Fanny Bullock, 45, 173, 181n
World War I
  efforts during: Marion Randall Parsons, 158, 176; Mary Roberts Rinehart, 120, 175, 186–87n; Grace Gallatin Seton, 86, 176; Elinore Pruitt Stewart, 106, 175
  start of, 174
  United States enters, 175
Wyeth, N. C., illustration by, *98*
Wyoming, women's firsts, 172, 176, 185n

Yosemite, 156, 179

Zumtaugwald, Gabriel, 44, 48–53